TWELVE MEN WHO CHANGED THE WORLD

The Apostles of Jesus Christ

Stanford E. Murrell

Ichthus Publications · Apollo, Pennsylvania

*"And he ordained twelve, that they
should be with him, and that he might
Send them forth to preach."*

—Mark 3:14

*"Go ye therefore, and teach all nations,
baptizing them in the name of the
Father, and of the Son, and of the Holy Ghost."*

—Matthew 28:19

Contents

1

A Sensitive Saint Named Simon Peter

"And he goeth up into a mountain, and calleth unto him whom he would: and they came unto him. [14] And he ordained twelve, that they should be with him, and that he might send them forth to preach, [15] And to have power to heal sicknesses, and to cast out devils: [16] And Simon he surnamed Peter; . . ." (Mark 3:13–21).

His body was slender and of a middle size, inclining to tallness. His complexion was pale and almost white. His beard was curled and thick, but short. His eyes were black, but flecked with red due to frequent weeping. Eyebrows thin, or none at all. This is the description from the ancient world of the man that is honored as St. Peter, the apostle of Jesus Christ. By way of introduction to the chief of the Master's men, several general facts should be noted. When we are first introduced to him, he is called Simon (Mark 1:16; John 1:40–41), a very popular name in the Jewish culture. We read of no less than nine Israelites in the Scriptures that bear this name.

- Simon Peter, the apostle of Jesus Christ.

1

- Simon the Zealot, another of the original Twelve Apostles (Matt. 10:4; Mark 3:18; Luke 6:15; Acts 1:13).

- Simon, a brother of James and Jude and Jesus—according to the flesh (Matt. 13:55; John 12:1–8).

- Simon the Leper, a resident of Bethany (Matt. 26:6–13; Mark 14:3–9; John 12:1–8).

- Simon of Cyrene, a Hellenistic Jew who was born on the north coast of Africa and was present at Jerusalem at the time of the crucifixion (cf. Acts 2:10).

- Simon the Pharisee in whose home a penitent woman washed the feet of Jesus with her tears and anointed them with oil (Luke 7:40, 43–44).

- Simon, the father of Judas Iscariot (John 6:71; 13:2, 26).

- Simon, the Samaritan magician, better known as Simon Magnus (Acts 8:5).

- Simon the Tanner, a Christian who lived in Joppa by the seashore (Acts 9:43; 10:6, 17, 32).

In honor of Simeon (lit. hearing), the second son of Jacob, devout Hebrew parents named their children.

Matthew records that one day as Jesus was walking along the shore of the Sea of Galilee, He saw two men fishing. They were brothers by birth and partners in trade by choice. One was named Simon, called Peter, and the other was Andrew. As Jesus watched the rugged fishermen, He noticed their serious faces and sturdy backs. Fishing for a living was no easy work. It required strong individuals with physical strength and mental stamina. Jesus needed such individuals to build His kingdom. Suddenly the Lord called out to the men who were dripping with water while laboring over their nets. Simon, Andrew, Follow me, and I will make you fishers of men.

That is all the Lord said for the moment, but it was enough. There was divine authority in that voice. The Sovereign Son of God had issued forth a personal summons and it was compelling enough to be obeyed. Immediately Simon dropped his work and he followed Christ. A series of questions soon emerged, no doubt, for Simon was a thinker as well as a talker. He wanted to know things, for his curiosity and enthusiasm was unbounded. What did Jesus mean by becoming fishers of men? What did it involve? When would the work begin? What kind of bait was to be used? Simon had so many things to inquire about, but he would have to be patient. All of his questions would be answered, but it would take time. For the moment, all that mattered was that Simon had entered into the greatest adventure of his life when he met Jesus. The Lord would change his heart, and then, through him, the Lord would change the world.

The first change had already taken place, as Christ changed Simon's occupation. From fishing for food that perishes, Simon would fish for the souls of men, and do a spiritual work that was to last forever. As the Lord changed His occupation, so He changed the Fisherman's name. John tells us how it happened in his gospel. One day Jesus gazed upon the strong disciple and said to him, "Thou art Simon the son of Jona, thou shalt be called Cephas, which is by interpretation, A stone" (John 1:42).

From being the son of a "fluttering, timorous dove," for such is the meaning of the name, Jona Simon would be a "solid rock," which is the meaning of the name Peter. But it would not be an easy transition; change never is. To fundamentally convert what a person is by nature requires a dramatic, and often traumatic, inner revolution. Peter would undergo such a revolution. He had to because by nature he was impulsive, which means that he often talked and acted first, and thought about the consequences later. This is not a criticism as much as an observation of comfort. Dr. F. B. Meyer makes this observation:

> Peter comes nearer to us than any of his brother apostles. We revere James, the brother of our Lord, for his austere saintliness. We strain our eyes in the effort to follow John to the serene heights, whither his eagle wing bore him. But Peter is so human, so like ourselves in his down-sittings and uprisings, so compassed with infirmity that we are encouraged to hope that perhaps the Great Potter may be able to make something even of our common clay.[1]

Despite his volatile personality there are some great things that can be noted about Peter.

First, there is The Moment of Illumination whereby Peter realizes that Jesus was the Messiah, the Son of the Living God. The Bible tells us precisely when this discovery was made. It was the third day after Peter met the Master. There was a marriage in Cana of Galilee, and the mother of Jesus was there. And both Jesus

---

[1] Quoted in the Foreword to F. B. Meyer, *Apostle Peter: Fisherman, Disciple, Apostle* (N.p.: Christian Publishing House, 2022).

was called, and his disciples to the marriage (John 2:1–11; cf. John 6:66–69; Matt. 16:18).

You are familiar with the story. The wedding feast ran low on wine. Mary appealed to her son to help her out of a socially embarrassing situation. The Lord helped His mother by turning water into wine. And the Bible says, "This beginning of miracles did Jesus in Cana of Galilee, and manifested forth His glory; and his disciples believed on Him" (John 2:11). In a moment of time, Peter learned that Jesus was the Christ, the Son of the Living God, and the Messiah that was to come. It was a Great Discovery.

Second, there is The Great Covenant whereby Peter was told that, in a specialized way, he would be the foundation of the church. The words of Jesus are very plain (Matt. 16:18). Thou art Peter and upon this rock I will build my church.

It is customary for conservative Bible commentators to be dogmatic in trying to stress a play on words in this verse by appealing to the original language so that the second word for rock (petra; a mass of rock) refers to Christ and not Peter (petros; a large piece of rock like a detached boulder). While anyone can be sympathetic to every effort to protect the honor of the Lord and His relationship to the Church, it is not necessary to reword biblical terminology, or church history. The truth of the matter is that the earliest records indicate that Jesus did indeed build His church upon Peter, as He said He would. The Lord honored His commitment. Even a casual reading of the Book of Acts will see that it happened as the Lord predicted.

It was Peter who preached on the Day of Pentecost and three thousand souls were saved (Acts 2:42).

It was Peter who suggested the selection of Matthias to take the place of Judas as an apostle (Acts 1:15–22). And while the outworking of that suggestion has a lot to be desired, it does show leadership among the brethren.

It was Peter who healed the lame beggar in the portico of the Temple saying, Silver and gold have I none, but such as I have, give I thee. In the name of Jesus Christ of Nazareth rise up and walk (Acts 3:4–6).

It was Peter who was falsely accused by the Rulers of the People and the Elders of the Council of Israel; and it was Peter who gave a defense of Christ (Acts 4:8–12, 29).

It was Peter who foretold the death by divine discipline of Ananias and Sapphira (Acts 5:1–11).

It was Peter who was imprisoned and scourged, and who had to give a second defense before the Jewish Council (Acts 5:17–42).

It was Peter who was first sent to Samaria as the Church expanded its missionary labors, and souls were brought into the Kingdom in obedience to the command of Christ (Acts 8:14).

It was Peter who prayed for the reception of the miraculous gifts of the Holy Spirit (Acts 8:15–18).

It was Peter who rebuked Simon, the sorcerer, when that greedy son of Satan desired to purchase the power of the Holy Spirit (Acts 8:18–24).

It was Peter who returned to Jerusalem to report on the great grace of God (Acts 8:25).

It was Peter who received Paul into the fellowship of the church and the work of the ministry (Gal.1:18; 2:9).

It was Peter who visited Lydda and healed Aeneas (Acts 9:32–34).

It was Peter who visited Joppa and stayed with Simon the tanner in order to raise Dorcas from the dead (Acts 9:36–43).

It was Peter who had a vision of a sheet containing ceremonially clean and unclean animals representing the Gentiles to whom the gospel was to be given (Acts 10:9–16).

It was Peter who received the servant of the centurion, ministered in Caesarea, preached to the centurion and his household, and in the middle of the night had a baptism service (Acts 10).

It was Peter who advocated the preaching of the gospel to the Gentiles in the hearing of the apostles and elders (Acts 11:1–18; 15:7–11).

It was Peter who, when imprisoned, was delivered by an angel (Acts 12:3–19).

It was Peter who wrote some of the earliest letters of the Bible.

It was Peter who told his story to a young man named John Mark, who wrote a gospel that bears his name.

The life of Peter is foundational in manifesting the visible church of Jesus Christ.

Of course, there is but One ultimate Foundation for the Church, as 1 Corinthians 3:11 teaches. For other foundation can no man lay than that which is laid, which is Jesus Christ. However, there is a secondary sense conveyed in the language of Matthew 16 and confirmed by Church history. The Lord really did fulfill His great promise to Peter. Upon his labors, in the power of the Holy Spirit, the Church was built in a visible manner (cf. Rev.

21:14; Eph. 2:20). Unfortunately, the Great Promise to Peter was followed by a Great Rebuke (Matt. 16:22, 23; Mark 8:32–33).

In context, Jesus had been speaking of His death. The very thought horrified Peter to the point that he began to emotionally reprimand the Lord. Peter did not want Christ to be associated with death and destruction. Jesus was the Son of Man. He was the Messiah that had been promised. He could overthrow the rulers of the world. He could govern supreme. With His divine powers, there was no limit to the kingdom that could come.

Peter wanted to be part of that dominion. He wanted Christ to live, and rule, and reign. And he wanted to be in the Cabinet of the King. In Peter's mind, Jesus must not suffer shame and reproach, and so he said, "Be it far from thee, Lord; this shall not be unto thee" (Matt. 16:22). Oh, Peter. You remind us once more that the best of men, are at best but men, and so are subject to spiritual blindness. Here was a shocking display of spiritual misunderstanding of the kingdom that Christ came to establish. Here was a tragic exposure of the fact that Peter did not yet comprehend the nature of the Person and the work that the Lord had come to perform. As a result, Christ moved to silence His servant. Turning rapidly upon Peter with a stormy look, Jesus uttered some of the most frightening words ever to fall upon the ears of a Saint, as He said, "Get thee behind me Satan: thou art an offense unto me: For thou savourest not the things that be of God, but Those that be of men" (Matt. 16:23).

Is it possible? Can Peter really be Satan? No, but the spirits of Satan and the philosophy of the Evil One was certainly present in the words of the apostle. The great objective of the Prince of

Darkness was to keep the Prince of Light from going to the Cross of Calvary and making atonement for sin. Many times, and in many ways, Jesus would be tempted to bypass the Cross for a crown. With the World, the Flesh, and the Devil against Him, Jesus did not need opposition and misunderstanding from Peter, and so the Lord administered the Severe Scolding.

Though spirits of Satan immediately left the scene of spiritual conflict, the Demons of Darkness still had their designs on Peter personally. They would return to influence his soul on another occasion, for we read of the Great Denial. As much as we would love to reconstruct the biblical narrative on this next matter to exonerate Simon Peter in some way, the truth of the matter is that Peter denied the Lord of Glory. And it happened this way:

> Now Peter sat without in the palace: and a damsel came unto him, saying Thou also wast with Jesus of Galilee. But he denied before them all, saying I know not what thou sayest. And when he was gone out into the porch, another maid saw him, and said unto them that were there, This fellow was also with Jesus of Nazareth. And again he denied with an oath, I do not know the man. And after a while came unto him they that stood by, and said to Peter, Surely thou also art one of them; for thy speech betrayeth thee. Then began he to curse and to swear, saying I know not the man. And immediately the cock crew. And Peter remembered the word of Jesus, which said unto him, Before the cock crows, thou shalt deny me thrice.

And he went out, and wept bitterly (Matt. 26:69–75).

In denying Christ publicly, Peter was no different from Judas Iscariot, who denied the Lord privately by selling information about Him to His enemies for thirty pieces of silver. To curse and deny the Lord of Glory is to betray His love and confidence. Peter, do you really not know the Man from Galilee? Peter, are you truly not one of His disciples? And Peter, instead of standing and identifying himself with the Accused, said I do not know Him. There was an Irrational Rejection.

But the story does not end, for there is the Righteous Return. Unlike Judas, Peter did repent of his sin in a genuine manner. The Bible does say that Judas repented of betraying Jesus. The Bible records the fact that Judas went to the synagogue and cast the blood money onto the floor, and then he went out and hung himself (Matt. 26:25ff). Judas repented but not in the same manner, nor for the same reason that Peter did (cf. Matt. 27:23), which tells us that there are different types of repentance.

There is the change of mind that says I made a terrible mistake, and there is the change of mind that cries out, God be merciful to me the sinner. The Bible says that when Judas saw that he was condemned for his action, he went out and hung himself. But when Peter comprehended what he had done, he went out and wept bitterly. His heart was genuinely broken. Jesus needed him and he had run away. A little girl pointed a finger at him, and the Rock turned to sand.

Here was no hero. Here was no Rock of Gibraltar. Here was no foundation upon which to build a house, let alone a church.

Here was a fearful heart. Here was a coward who cursed the Christ he wanted to crown.

Weep, Peter. Weep bitter tears. It is an awful deed that you have done. Somehow, Peter made it through the night of the crucifixion and the Sabbath that followed. Then came Sunday morning and a new day dawned that would forever alter the course of human history. Women came to tell Peter of an empty tomb and a resurrected Christ. Peter, the Lord has risen from among the dead! Run Peter! Run to the graveyard to see if it is true. Run Peter! Leave John behind in your haste to enter into the empty tomb and handle the burial clothes of the King of kings and Lord of lord who now wears the robes of Royalty (John 20:6). Jesus can leave the garments of death behind for He will need them no longer. Run Peter, run. Christ is alive.

And, Peter, the Lord wants to see you. He has asked for you personally. It is true, Peter. Holy angels instructed Mary Magdalene and Mary, the mother of Jesus, and Salome, saying to them when they reached the tomb, Go your way, tell His disciples, and Peter, that He goeth before you unto Galilee: there shall ye see Him, as He said unto you.

Peter went to Galilee and there he found Jesus, The Great Lover of Souls. The Lord had something He wanted Peter to do. He wanted Peter to feed His sheep (John 21:1–19). Three times the Lord told Peter, Feed my sheep. And he did. For the rest of his life, Peter fed the sheep as he followed the Great Shepherd and the Savior of his soul. Never again did Peter curse Christ or turn away from Him, although according to legend, there was a final opportunity to do that. According to one account by Hegesippus, when persecution broke out in A.D. 64 under Nero, Peter was back in Rome. By this time, he had preached the gospel far and wide in such places as Britain and Gaul (France), but then he returned to Rome. As the leader of the Christian community that did not worship the Emperor, who thought himself to be God, Peter was arrested by Nero and thrown into the Mamertine dungeon for nine months.

Prior to being arrested, Peter had a chance to flee the city, as many Christians wanted him to do. At last he was persuaded and made preparations to leave. But arriving at the gate, Peter saw the Lord Jesus coming to meet him, to whom he said, Lord, whither dost Thou go? And Jesus answered, and said, I am come again to be crucified. By this, Peter, perceiving his own sufferings were in view, returned into the city. Jerome said that Peter was crucified on an X-shaped cross, his head being down and his feet upward, by his own request, because he told his tormentors that he was not worthy to be crucified after the same form and die in the same manner as the Lord Jesus Christ.

There is much more that could be, and should be said about Peter. A single characteristic will have to suffice. The Great Sensitivity of Peter's Soul should not be overlooked. The sensitive soul of Peter is reflected in his hospitality. It was in the home of Peter that Jesus often went to rest from His labors. One of the great virtues of the Christian life is to be given to hospitality. In fact, it is so important that the Holy Spirit makes it a qualification for church leadership (1 Tim. 3:2).

Again, the sensitive soul of Simon Peter is reflected in his intense sense of sin. It was Peter who once said, "Depart from me, O

Lord, for I am a sinful man" (Luke 5:8). And it was Peter who once wept bitter tears of repentance after receiving only a look from Jesus. One look from the eyes of Jesus could always bring Peter back to the way of honor and fidelity.[2]

It would be good if the soul of every saint was as sensitive to sin as Peter's. We need such a heart to beat in us because we are living in a cold and cruel country, reflected in the ever-increasing random acts of violence. Neighbors do not know one another, and families are torn apart. Nations are at war, and individuals feel isolated. Many are filled with hatred and hostility. The Church has an opportunity to show kindness and sensitivity to others in a sin-saturated society. Indeed, Christ calls upon His Church to care. It was St. Francis of Assisi, who prayed,

> Lord, make me an instrument of your peace.
> Where there is hatred, let me sow love;
> Where there is injury, pardon;
> Where there is doubt, faith;
> Where there is despair, hope;
> Where there is darkness, light;
>
> And where there is sadness, joy.
> O Divine Master,
> Grant that I may not so much seek
> To be consoled as to console;
> To be understood as to understand;
> To be loved as to love.

---

[2] See William Barclay, *The Master's Men.*

For it is in giving that we receive,
It is in pardoning that we are pardoned,
And it is in dying that we are born to eternal life.

By God's grace, we want be sensitive enough to love and to care. We want to cry with those who cry, and laugh with those who are laughing. And, by God's grace, we want to be sensitive to sin in ourselves so that we can pray to the Lord and say with sincerity: When thou see'est me waver, with a look, recall.

2

James: The Son of Zebedee

"Now about that time Herod the king stretched forth his hands to vex certain of the church. ²And he killed James the brother of John with the sword" (Acts 12:1–2).

The resurrection of Jesus Christ from the dead gave strength and courage to the Apostles to boldly proclaim the message of redeeming grace. Before the resurrection there was nothing but despair. But afterwards, the fearful followers of Christ became the most courageous individuals in the world, which is one good reason to believe in the resurrection of Christ. Something changed the disciples from being timid, to spiritual tigers, and that something was a historical event. John R. W. Stott says: "Perhaps the transformation of the disciples of Jesus is the greatest evidence of all for the resurrection. On the day of the crucifixion, the disciples had been filled with sadness; but on the first day of the week they were filled with gladness. Why? Something radical happened to change them forever. Jesus was alive! Salvation was to be proclaimed to all."

Beginning at Jerusalem, the gospel was preached until the message of the Master traveled to the whole world. But it was not easy to present a new message because the gospel of Christ challenged long established beliefs and traditions in both the Gentile and Jewish communities. In particular, the gospel proclaimed that only Jesus was Lord. The Romans viewed that particular religious conviction as a direct assault upon imperial patriotism, for the Christians began to refuse to pay any tribute to the Emperor as Master or Lord. Christ is Lord, they said, and did not yield the point. Rome was resentful.

In the Jewish community, the proclamation that Christ was the promised Messiah was unwanted, in part, because of economic reasons. If the message was true, then it meant that Judaism, with all of its elaborate priesthood and sacrificial system, was obsolete. Culturally, an ancient way of life would be overthrown. Thousands of jobs were at stake if the Shadow of things to come had to give way to the Substance.

There was no need to buy or sell animals for sacrifice. There was no need for all the butchers. There was no need for the vendors that sold their wares to the Jews who came to Jerusalem on the three most sacred days of the year.

So much could be done away with if Christ was the Son of the Living God and the Savior of the world. It is not difficult to understand why Christians were not tolerated in Roman or Jewish communities. Wherever they went, their message created social unrest as the claims of Christ were presented. Of course, the real issue that was at stake in the encounters of Christians with the world was not patriotism, job opportunities, or even religious toleration, but ultimate truth. If Jesus was the Way, the Truth, and the Life, then not only His deity was established, but also His sovereignty, and that would put an obligation upon people to repent of their sins, worship and obey Him. For many, that was unacceptable, and still is.

One of the great reasons why people do not want to believe in Jesus Christ as Lord and Savior is because of some moral issue. Josh McDowell tells of counseling a student who was fed up with Christianity, because she believed it was not historical, and there was just nothing to it factually. She had convinced everyone that she had searched and found profound intellectual problems as the result of her university studies. One person after another would try to persuade her intellectually, and to answer her many accusations. I listened, said Josh, and then asked several questions. Within 30 minutes she admitted she had fooled everyone, and that she developed these intellectual doubts in order to excuse her moral life.

Many years ago, southern evangelist Dr. John R. Rice suggested that at the root of every doctrinal error there is a moral failure. Perhaps he is right. Immorality and false doctrine often go hand in hand. There are many reasons why people reject Christ. One of them is an unwillingness to give up an improper lifestyle. Two thousand years ago, those who initially heard the gospel listened, and understood its implications and divided into two groups, those for Christ and those against Him. That is still the only division possible today. There is no neutrality. Jesus said, He that is not with me is against me; and he that gathereth not with Me scattereth abroad (Matt.12:30). Those who opposed Christ in the

First Century A.D. had to discredit the Messiah and His messengers. Certainly they tried.

Vicious accusations were hurled against Jesus personally. Some said He was illegitimate. Some said that He was a drunkard. Some said that He was a Friend of the lowest class of people. Some said that He cast out demons by the power of Beelzebub. Some said that He was not in His right mind.

In like manner, vicious accusations were hurled against the followers of Christ. The Christians were accused of paganism, for they believed in only one God, as opposed to the many gods of the Romans. The Christians were accused of immorality, for they held Love Feasts. The Christians were accused of cannibalism, for they ate the body and drank the blood of their Leader. The Christians were accused of being unpatriotic and causing sedition, for they would not offer a pinch of incense, and declare that Caesar was Lord. In the year of our Lord, A.D. 44, Herod Agrippa I charged one Christian, in particular, with political insurrection. His name was James, the son of Zebedee.

Agrippa I was a son of Aristobulus, and grandson of King Herod the Great, who was the ruler of Palestine when Christ was born. Following the execution of his infamous father in 7 B.C., Agrippa was brought up in Rome as a member of the royal family, which means that he was spoiled.

In A.D. 23 he was so far in debt that he had to leave the city. For a while, his Uncle Antipas sustained him at Tiberias at the request of his sister Herodias, whom Antipas had recently married. But as might be expected, he argued with Antipas, and in A.D. 36 returned to Rome. There, Agrippa managed to offend the Emperor Tiberius, and was imprisoned. However, a year after the death of Tiberius he was released by the new emperor of Rome, Gaius (Caligula).

Though he would eventually go insane, Caligula gave Agrippa the title of king, with territories northeast of Palestine as his kingdom. With the passing of time, and despite the civil turmoil of Rome's national government, Agrippa increased his local base of political power. When Claudius became emperor in A.D. 41, he gave Agrippa the rule over Judea and Samaria. Wanting to find favor with his Jewish subjects, Agrippa discovered that persecuting the Christians was a popular thing to do. And so he stretched forth his hands to vex certain of the Church. And he killed James, the brother of John with the sword (Acts 12:1–2).

Agrippa should not have touched the Lord's anointed. Three years later, in A.D. 44, He died suddenly the death of the wicked. At the age of 54, Agrippa unexpectedly stepped out of time and into eternity because he gave not God the glory: and he was eaten of worms, and gave up the ghost (Acts 12:20ff). The name Agrippa I will forever be associated with spiritual acts of infamy, for he persecuted the Church, arrested Peter, and killed James. Seventeen years had passed between the call that James received from the Master, and the martyrdom he suffered for Him.

James is first introduced in the biblical narrative in partnership with his brother John, and his father Zebedee. Apparently the fishing business on the Lake of Galilee was prosperous, for the family employed hired servants (Mark 1:19–20). There were other signs of personal wealth. The family owned a house in Jerusalem and enjoyed social status. They were known to be friends of the

High Priest, Caiaphas, and his household. Zebedee was in the habit of frequently visiting the home (John 18:15–16). However, there came a day when James, and his brother John, left a position of privilege and prestige to follow Christ. Into the apostolic band James and John went, and with Peter, a close friend, formed an inner circle around Jesus, so that they were with the Lord on the most sacred occasions, and the most memorable moments of His ministry.

- They were with Jesus at the raising of the daughter of Jarius (Mark 5:37; Luke 8:51).
- They were with Jesus at the transfiguration (Matt. 17:1; Mark 9:2; Luke 9:28).
- They were with Jesus during the Lord's agony in the Garden of Gethsemane (Mark 14:33; Matt. 26:37).

It is interesting to note that these three disciples (James, John, and Peter), who were to suffer so much for the cause of Christ, should witness the raising of the dead, to give them courage to die; the transfiguration of Christ that they might know the reality of the spiritual world; and the agony in the Garden that they might understand that they too must suffer agony for Christ.[3] Jesus had predicted that James and John would share in His sufferings. The Lord had promised that they would drink of the same cup that He had to drink (Matt. 20:22–23; Mark 10:35–39). They did, but in different ways.

---

[3] See Barclay, *The Master's Men.*

John went to Ephesus to minister. He lived about a hundred years, and died. The life of James came to a brutal end much earlier than that of John, and yet they both drank from the cup of the Lord. If this sounds contradictory, that one should die young, and the other old, that one should die by violence, and the other die in old age, if this appears to be an annulment of the promise of Christ, perhaps an illustration will help.

There was a Roman coin that had on its inscription the picture of an ox facing an altar, and a plough with the words, Ready for Either. That was James and that was John. They were ready for either, the altar, or the plough. They were ready for either selfless sacrifice, or tedious toil, in the service of the Savior. And so they were like the Lord, and drank from His cup. In like manner all Christians must be ready for either. The Lord still asks some individuals to go to the altar, others are left behind to toil for a time.

The Bible tells us plainly that James gave his neck meekly to the sword of the lictor at the command of a mad ruler. He was beheaded at Jerusalem. James could go as a sheep to the slaughter because a wonderful transformation in his character had taken place. We have an insight into just how deeply the transformation touched James, for in Mark 3:17 he is called, with John, Boanerges, which means, "the sons of thunder." The name speaks of fiery zeal, boundless energy, and a volatile personality. James was the type of person that was prone to overreact to a given situation. It was his tendency to bring incredible pressure to any situation in order that he might prevail. James was not a man that you would want to cross. We know that from Luke 9:51–56.

In context, an incident is recorded in which a group of Samaritans seemed to slight Jesus and the apostles. Outraged at the rejection, James and John asked, no doubt in all sincerity, Lord, will thou that we command fire to come down from heaven, and consume them, even as Elijah did? There is no doubt that if the Lord had not subdued the passion of His disciples they would have called fire down from heaven to destroy their enemies and been more than happy to do it. There are people who will hurt others, given the opportunity. But God has called His people to peace. There were several things fundamentally wrong with the thinking of James and John in this incident.

First, Holy Scripture was being misunderstood and misused. While it is true that Elijah called down unusual and harsh judgment upon some individuals, it was simply in confirmation of a divine judicial judgment that had already been passed because of the worship of idols. The situation in Elijah's day was quite different from wanting to kill people because of a social slight.

Second, the suddenness of the anger of James and John was wrong. They were immediately irritated at a moment in time, and they lashed out. It is a terrible thing to allow irritability to rule so that raw anger is unleashed, and irrational words are spoken that destroy relationships. James reminds us that words are not neutral. They communicate concrete ideas, and emotions, and elicit a response in kind.

Jesus was right to sharply rebuke the disciples and remind them that they knew not what spirit they were of. Anger is a spiritual matter. Christians are called upon to guard not only what is said, but also the spirit in which something is said. Sarcasm, ridicule, and mockery, can be replaced with sensitivity, respect, and mercy. The poet encourages us to speak better things with this simple prayer:

> If any little words of ours
>> Can make one life the brighter;
> If any little song of ours
>> Can make one heart the lighter;
>
> God help us speak that little word,
>> And take our bit of singing
> And drop it in some lonely vale
>> To set the echoes ringing.

James, the son of Zebedee, the passionate brother of John, did learn to speak the little words that helped people. He renounced the harsh words that threatened to hurt. Even in the hour of his death, James was gentle. Eusebius, the early Church historian, records that the Roman guard who led James to the judgment seat saw him bearing his Christian testimony well in the hour of personal pain, and imminent death. Arriving at the place of execution, the guard suddenly declared his own faith in Christ to the judge and begged James to forgive him. And he, after considering a little, said, Peace be with thee, and kissed him. And thus they were both beheaded at the same time.

James went to the grave being used of the Lord to bring others to salvation.

James was faithful unto death.

But while he lived, James lived with passion and zeal for the Savior having been tempered in anger, tempered in prejudice, and tempered in personal ambition. May the Lord allow all within the Church the privilege of doing the same.

General Facts and Practical Application
About the Apostles of Christ

In all four lists of the apostles, James, the son of Zebedee, is always cited among the first three apostles listed.

His mother's name was Salome. She, too, was a believer in Christ, and in His coming kingdom (Matt. 20:20). So much did Salome believe in the Lord, that she ambitiously asked for places of honor to be given to her sons. When it appeared that the hope of an earthly kingdom had vanished with the arrest of Christ, Salome still followed the Lord. She followed Him to the Cross, and beyond that, to the tomb. Salome was there on the resurrection morning to discover the Living Lord (Mark 15:40; 16:1).

The father of James, Zebedee, was not a follower of Christ, as far as the gospel record reveals. The Bible does present him as being financially prosperous through his fishing business, and socially prominent. But not a Christian. It may have been that the family members were divided over Jesus. It happens far too often.

In the matter of following Christ, James sided with his mother, and was forever grateful for a great lady of grace, for Jesus changed his life in three areas.

The Lord subdued his zeal. James as we have seen was over-zealous. He was like Jehu in the Old Testament, who said,

Come...see my zeal for the Lord. But even religious zeal needs to be tempered if it is used to hurt, and not to help others.

The Lord subdued his racial prejudices against non-Israelites, such as the Samaritans and other Gentiles. To a devout Jew, the Samaritan was a dog; but to Christ, the Samaritans were subjects for salvation (John 5).

The Lord subdued the ambition of James. James wanted to sit on a throne. He was given the privilege of bearing a martyr's testimony and of learning that unbridled ambition has no place in the Kingdom of Heaven. Shakespeare wrote about "Vaulting ambition which o'er leaps itself, And falls on the other."[4]

Having learned that, James did receive a throne to sit upon. Jesus promised, To him that overcometh, will I grant to sit with me in my throne, Even as I also overcame, and am set down with my Father in His throne (Rev. 3:21; cf. 22:3–5).

Because Christ transformed James, he was able to be of great practical use in the work of the ministry. In fact, James became a prominent leader in the early church, reflected in the fact that he was the first apostle to receive a martyr's crown. His life and his death become a clarion call to all men, in every generation, to serve the Savior.

> Rise up, O men of God! Have done with lesser things;
> Give heart and mind and soul and strength
> To serve the King of kings.

---

[4] *Macbeth*, Act 1, scene 7.25–28.

Rise up, O men of God! His kingdom tarries long;
  Bring in the day of brother-hood
And end the night of wrong.

Rise up, O men of God! The Church for you doth wait,
  Her strength unequal to her task; Rise up and make her
  great.
Lift high the Cross-of Christ! Tread where His feet have
  trod;
As brothers of the Son of man, Rise up, O men of God![5]

---

[5] William Pierson Merrill.

3

John: A Son of Thunder and a Brother of Love

"And James the son of Zebedee, and John the brother of James; and he surnamed them Boanerges, which is, The sons of thunder:" (Mark 3:17).

"What say you, friends? That this is John of Ephesus who has gone back to His kingdom? Aye, 'tis so, 'tis so; I know it all: and yet, just now I seemed to stand once more upon my native hills and touch my Master. Up! Bear me to my church once more. There let me tell them of a Savior's love: For by the sweetness of my Master's voice I think He must be very near. So raise up, my head: How dark it is! I cannot seem to see the faces of my flock. Is that the sea that murmurs so, or is it weeping? Hush my little children. God so loved the world He gave His Son: So love ye one another, Love God and men. Amen. With these words, the poet Eastwood described the last hours of St. John's life, and what a life it was. The gospel narrative introduces John as one of the sons of Zebedee, a fisherman of Galilee. When not engaged in the hard work of the fishing trade, John, along with his friend Andrew, would go to hear the zealous preacher called John the Baptist (John 1:34–40). What eventful days they were that John spent amid the crowd at Jordan, as he listened to the mighty preaching of the Baptist who had caught something of the spirit and power of Elijah! How deeply impressed John was by the strong character and forceful teaching of the Baptist!" (Herbert Lockyer).

Then, one day, into the presence of John the Baptist, Jesus walked. The Man Sent from God, the one who ate locust and wild honey and spoke with the voice of ultimate spiritual authority, gazed with blazing eyes upon Christ. Suddenly pointing to Him, the Baptist cried out saying (John 1:29), Behold the Lamb of God that taketh away the sin of the world. John, the son of Zebedee, first looked, and then he followed the Lamb. It was a glorious consolation for John to see Him whom kings and prophets longed to see (Matt. 13:17; Luke 10:24; Heb. 11:13). Augustine wished to see Solomon in his glory, Paul in the pulpit, and Christ in the flesh. In the pastoral exhortation of John the Baptist, to look to Christ, every word is significant.

Behold! Here is a summons to the world, to look to Christ. Whatever your need may be, look to Christ. We are not told to look neither to science, nor to psychology, nor even to self. We must look to Christ. Here is a summary of the gospel ministry. We preach not ourselves, but Christ Jesus the Lord (2 Cor. 4:5). Behold the object of faith.

The Lamb. John could have said, Look to the King of kings and Lord of lords. He could have said, Behold the Sovereign of the universe. He could have said, Behold the Judge of all righteousness, but John said, Behold, the Lamb. This was the name given by the Holy Spirit to mark Him out as The Sacrifice. Isaiah 53:7, "He was oppressed, and he was afflicted, yet he opened not his mouth"; he is brought as a lamb to the slaughter, and as a sheep before her shearers is dumb, so he openeth not his mouth. The emblem of the Lamb was chosen because it speaks of innocence, meekness, and patience (1 Pet. 1:19; Rev. 5:5). But this was no ordinary Lamb. It was the Lamb of God.

The Lamb of God. This Hebraism speaks of three things. First, the Lamb was foreordained of God. God never intended that the sacrificial lambs of the Jews should be offered forever. They were all significant by way of typology, but insufficient by way of a Divine satisfaction for sin. All the thousands of lambs slain from the hour of deliverance from Egypt could give the conscience of men no rest. All the Paschal lambs ever eaten could not satisfy the hungering spirit. Only the Lamb whom God the Father foreordained could do that.

Second, the Lamb of God speaks of a Lamb well pleasing to God. The Father was well pleased, because the Lamb did not resist His will, but always did what the Father asked. The Father was well pleased, because the Lamb would give value to all previous sacrifices pledged. The Lamb would confirm that God keeps His word, and honors His covenants to men (Gen. 3:15).

Third, the Lamb of God reflects the most tender relationship conceivable to God. God told the world that He was coming to them, not in wrath but in love and tenderness, for a stated purpose: To take (bear) away the sin of the world. Sin is a great burden to bear. Its tremendous weight lies heavy upon the human heart. Who can endure the crushing magnitude of sin? It will ultimately sink the guilty soul into the depth of hell. Someone is needed to take this burden away. Someone is needed to bear the sin of the world. Behold that Someone! Behold the Lamb of God!

Notice what the Lamb will do. He will take away sin. He will do this by shedding His blood, for without the shedding of blood there is no remission of sin (Heb. 9:22).

By shedding His blood the Lamb will make atonement for sin. The atonement will appease the Divine justice of God, and turn away His wrath from all those who are covered by the shed blood of the Lamb. Those who are covered by the blood of the Lamb, are those who by faith look to Christ as the Savior of the world. Do you understand? The Sacrifice, the Lamb of God, is a Savior. He came to bare our sins in His own body on the tree. He was made a curse for us. He is a complete Savior. He finished His work and by one offering hath perfected forever them who are sanctified. He is a mighty Savior. Jew or Gentile, rich or poor, male or female, young or old, He ever liveth to make intercession. He is a perpetual Savior. Not merely has the Lamb taken away the sin of those souls who call Him Lord, but He still bears them away, a continuous present tense: He taketh away the sin of the world. Does that mean that all people shall be saved? No, but it does mean that all those in the world who shall lay hold of Christ, by faith, shall be saved with certainty, and finality.

Is it any wonder that John began to travel with the Lamb of God, and that he followed the Lamb wherever He went? And so, John was with Jesus during His first tour of Galilee. He was with the Lord at the wedding in Cana (John 2:1ff), and he was present at Jerusalem during the Lord's early Judean ministry. John never wavered, and he never went home. Wherever Jesus was, John could be found nearby. As the Gospel narrative unfolds, there are several distinct elements that emerge about John.

First, he was a personable individual. There was something about John that attracted attention and made people want to be around him. Before long, John was numbered with the select inner group that was with Jesus during important moments. With Peter and James, John was present at the raising of the daughter of Jarius (Mark 5:27), and at the transfiguration (Matt. 17). During the agony of Christ in Gethsemane, John was nearby. He was sleeping, but he was there.

Second, John was a man of great passion. There was intensity in his personality that earned him the nickname, along with his brother, Sons of Thunder. Unfortunately, his passion was often misguided. In Mark 3:17, John wanted to destroy a Samaritan village because the people there refused the Lord and His disciples hospitality.

On another occasion, John expressed his zeal, as well as his intolerance and exclusiveness, when he informed Jesus, Therefore, we saw one casting out demons in thy name; and we forbade him, because he followed not us (Mark 9:38). Thinking to be commended for his action, John was instead rebuked, as the Lord responded, "Forbid him not: for there is no man, which shall do a miracle in my name, that can lightly speak evil of me. For he that is not against us is on our part. For whosoever shall give you a cup of water to drink in my name, because ye belong to Christ, verily I say unto you, he shall not lose his reward" (Mark 9:39–41).

There is a *third* thing we learn about John. He was a man of high ambition. Perhaps it was because he had already tasted of the success of this world that he went with his mother and his brother to ask a favor of the Lord. He did not ask for much. He only wanted the highest place of honor when Christ came into His kingdom (Mark 10:35). But Jesus said, No, to that request.

It is instructive to note that while on that occasion the Lord had to rebuke the passion of selfish ambition, at the Last Supper John did occupy a privileged place of intimacy next to Jesus (John 13:23). The Lord does not deny honor to people. He simple wants His servants to wait to be exalted.

A *fourth* characteristic of John is that he was a man of faith. Perhaps his greatest expression of faith came when he saw the empty tomb, and beheld the grave clothes. He saw, and believed (John 20:8). Never again would John ever weaken as to whom Jesus Christ was and what He came to do. For the rest of his life John was a preacher of righteousness. Initially, John united with Peter for the work of proclaiming the gospel. John was with Peter at the Gate of the Temple when a lame man was healed (Acts 3:10). He was also with Peter on the mission to Samaria to speak to the new converts (Acts 8:12).

Besides being a preacher of righteousness, John was also a defender of the faith. It was not long before heresy arose in the early church. Heresy is basically truth mixed with error to a great degree. According to the Church father Jerome, John wrote the gospel in order to combat the heresy of Cerinthus. Cerinthus was teaching the Gnostic heresy that Jesus was not God. He asserted that Christ did not exist before Mary, and when Jesus was born it was only an appearance. His death was only apparent, not real. It was said that if Jesus walked along the sandy shores of the sea, His feet would leave no imprint for He was not true humanity. So it was that John wrote, "In the beginning was the Word, and the Word was with God, and the Word was God. And the Word was made flesh and dwelt among us, (and we beheld his glory, the glory as of the only begotten of the Father) full of grace and truth."

Despite the seriousness of Gnosticism, and the heresy of Cerinthus, Church history does contain a rather humorous incident as recorded by Eusebius. John, the Apostle, once entered a public bath to wash: but, ascertaining Cerinthus was within, he ran out of the place and fled from the door, not enduring to remain under the same roof with him. John exhorted those within to do the same, Let us flee lest the bath fall in, as long as Cerinthus, that enemy of the truth, is within. The image of an apostle running out of a public bathhouse, dripping wet, while clutching his clothes, is not the most dignified of images, but it does serve to illustrate John's passion for purity of doctrine, and his willingness to personally avoid heretics.

Tradition records something else about John. Not only did he defend his faith, but he was willing to suffer for it as well. Legend says that John first faced martyrdom when he was boiled in a huge basin of bubbling oil during a surge of official persecution in Rome. In a miraculous way, he survived the ordeal. Later, John was banished to the isle of Patmos as a political activist. While on Patmos, John looked out towards the mainland and longed to be with his church family again. Perhaps the apostle was thinking about that when he wrote in the Book of the Revelation that in the redeemed earth, there was no more sea, by which he means there will be no more separations from those we love in the Lord. After being freed, he returned to serve as Bishop of Edessa in modern Turkey.

On the 26th day of September, c. A.D. 100, John died peacefully. Before his death his disciples had gathered around him. As was his custom, John told them again, "Little children, love one another." After a while his disciples grew weary of this single command repeated over and over. Master, one of them asked. Why do you always say this? And John replied, "It is the Lord's command. And if this alone be done, it is enough!" With that, the man of passion, the man of ambition, the man of faith, the preacher of righteousness, and the apostle of love, died.

From his life we can learn many things. *First*, a particular type of personality does not prohibit a person from entering into the kingdom of heaven, or being used of God. While the Lord might have to transform our temperament, there is always hope that God can use any type of disposition in His service.

Second, a teachable spirit is characteristic of true discipleship. Part of being teachable is a willingness to receive instruction, even if it takes the form of a rebuke. On several occasions Jesus had to rebuke John, who was humbled under the rod of corrective discipline. It is not easy to learn when under the rod, but if God grants grace there will be much value.

Third, humility is of great virtue. Despite the fact that we have more of John's writing than any other apostle, there is very little autobiographical material. Sometimes he is called, "The disciple whom Jesus loved" (John 13:23; 20:2; 21:7, 10), but beyond that it is Christ, not John, who is set forth.

Fourth, the life of John teaches Christians that love must be a guiding passion. To be loving, and to love, is the highest virtue of Christendom. To love God and one's fellowman is the summary of the Law. And if we do that, it really is enough.

4

Andrew: The Man with a Passion for Souls

"Accept me, O Christ Jesus,
Whom I saw, whom I love,
And in whom I am;
Accept my spirit in peace
In your eternal realm."

According to tradition, it was with this final prayer upon his lips that St. Andrew departed this life to enter into the glories of heaven. The Bible does not tell us much about Andrew, but what it does record is significant. From John 1:44, it is discovered Andrew was a native of Bethsaida. Josephus, the Jewish historian, describes the general area as a rich and beautiful place producing an abundance of diverse crops. Fishing was also an important industry.

Like so many other men of his day, Andrew was the son of a fisherman named Jonah (John). Following in the family tradition, Andrew became a fisherman with his brother Peter. He flung his net into the Sea of Galilee in order to harvest the fish for food. It was hard work, requiring long hours of toil and labor.

While there is nothing wrong with that, there is spiritual danger even in honest labor. It is possible for the daily routines of life to become a strain on a person, dulling all sense of sensitivity of the soul. It is possible to become so busy in life doing valid things that there is no time for the Eternal. Therefore, it needs to be said: the person who works only for work's sake is a sad individual indeed, for man is made to be more than a beast of burden. Some people must be warned to find a way to relax in their labors, lest they destroy themselves, and harm others. The principle of rest is established in the Ten Commandments.

> Remember the Sabbath day, to keep it holy. Six days shalt thou labor, and do all thy work: But the seventh day is the Sabbath of the Lord thy God: in it thou shalt not do any work, thou, nor thy son, nor thy daughter, thy manservant, nor thy maidservant, nor thy cattle, nor thy stranger that is within thy gates: For in six days the Lord made heaven and earth, the sea, and all that in them is, and rested the seventh day: wherefore the Lord blessed the Sabbath day, and hallowed it (Exodus 20:8–11).

Man is more than a muscle. He has a soul and spirit, as well as a body, and he must cultivate an appreciation for the esthetics of life. Art and music, literature and drama, meditation and worship, must balance out the physical labors of life. Following World War I, the wife of an American Foreign Service Officer living in Germany invited the American novelist Thornton Wilder, to come and speak in a small university town in Germany. In a telegram, she sent this message: We need you here where everyone has forgotten how to think, not having for a long time been permitted to think. We need to be told again that poets are a little above kings, and not at all below the saints, because nobody here remembers this anymore.

Andrew would have understood that telegram because there beat in his breast a hope for heaven. Andrew, the rugged fisherman, was also a man who wanted more meaning to life than the mere routine of hauling in boatloads of fish to sell on the open market. That is why, when John the Baptist appeared preaching that the kingdom of heaven was at hand, Andrew left Bethsaida to hear the message of the man in the wilderness of Judea.

Andrew walked a long way down the Jordan Valley (50–60 miles) to come to the place where John was preaching at Bethany, across the Jordan from Jericho. John preached a message of repentance as he said: I am the voice of one crying in the wilderness, Make straight the way of the Lord, as said the prophet Esaias (John 1:28). As Isaiah called people to repentance, so did John. But what does that mean? What is repentance? Formally, according to the *Westminster Shorter Catechism*, "Repentance unto life is a saving grace, whereby a sinner, out of a true sense of his sin, and apprehension [that is, laying hold] of the mercy of God in Christ, does, with grief and hatred of his sin, turn from it unto God, with full purpose of, and endeavor after, new obedience."

Specifically, biblical repentance involves a turning away from sin, a turning away from active, willful disobedience and rebellion, and a turning back to God (Matt. 9:13; Luke 5:32). There are many people who are living in open and active revolt against the

Lord. Some of them are Christians. The gospel calls upon individuals to turn around and stop any arrogant assault upon Divine authority.

In a more general sense, repentance means a change of mind (Gen. 6:6–7) because of a feeling of remorse, or regret, for past or present conduct (Matt. 27:3). True repentance is a godly sorrow for sin. True repentance involves recognizing that I have sinned against the God of heaven, who is great and gracious, holy and loving, and that I am not worthy to be called His son, says Albert N. Martin. In the Old Testament, the classic case of repentance is that of King David, after Nathan the prophet accused him of killing Uriah the Hittite and committing adultery with Uriah's wife, Bathsheba. David's prayer of repentance for this sin is found in Psalm 51. I suspect that many teardrops fell upon that first manuscript, for David knew something about godly sorrow. He was sick over his sins.

Turning to the New Testament, we find out something else about repentance. John the Baptist called upon individuals, to Repent, for the kingdom of heaven is at hand (Matt. 3:2), and then he went on to tell the multitudes, to Bear fruits worthy of repentance (Matt. 3:8; Luke 3:8). Biblical repentance produces a spiritual change of life. It is not enough to ask for God's forgiveness, if the time never comes to depart from that which is wrong in order to do what is right.

A lot of people might admit that something is wrong in their lives, but they have not yet repented. They have not yet decided to do what is right. When true repentance takes place, it will produce works of righteousness.

Meaningful prayer *1 Kings 8:47*

Faith *Mark 1:15*

Obedience to gospel duties (such as baptism) *Acts 2:38*

Humility *Matthew 11:21*

A turning from willful sin *1 John 3:6*

Speaking to the believers at Trinity Baptist Church in Montville, N. J., Dr. Albert N. Martin had this to say: It is rather pointed and straightforward. Maybe some of you are involved in fornication, or in heavy petting, or in looking at the kind of stuff on television and in the movies that feeds your lust, and yet you name the name of Christ. You live in the hog pens and then go to a house of God on Sunday. Shame on you! Leave your hog pens and your haunts of sin. Leave your patterns and practices of fleshly and carnal indulgence. Repentance is being sorry enough to quit your sin. You will never know the forgiving mercy of God while you are still wedded to your sins. Jesus warned, Unless you repent, you will all likewise perish (Luke 13:3, 5). This is the negative or judgmental side of repentance. The positive or merciful side is seen in other words, such as those found in Luke 16:10: There is joy in the presence of the angels of God over one sinner who repents. That is what the Lord wants. He wants people to come to faith and live a happy and wholesome life of godliness.

After the crucifixion and resurrection of Christ, the Lord's disciples continued to proclaim His message of repentance and faith (Acts 2:38; 3:19; 20:21; 26:20). They, too, taught that repentance is a turning from wickedness and dead works (Acts 8:22; Heb. 6:1) toward God and His glory (Acts 20:21; Rev. 16:9) resulting in eternal life (Acts 11:18) while growing in knowledge of the truth (2 Tim. 2:25). Repentance is God's will and pleasure (Luke 15:7–10; 2 Pet. 3:9) as well as His command (Mark 6:12; Acts 17:30). It is a gift of His sovereign love (Acts 5:31; 11:18; Rom. 2:4; 2 Tim. 2:25) without which we cannot be saved (Luke 13:3).

Andrew repented. He was willing to make straight the way of the Lord, and so it was that when the Lord of Glory appeared before Him in Person on the bank of the Jordan River, Andrew was ready to move toward Him, and embrace Him. Behold, said John, the Lamb of God which taketh away the sin of the world (John 1:29). Andrew beheld the Lamb, and he never took his eyes off of Christ. According to the gospel narrative, Andrew was the first of all the twelve to identify himself with Jesus. The early church realized this, and often called Andrew the *protokletos*, which literally means, First-called.

Not only did Andrew identify himself with Jesus, but he introduced others to the Lord as well. Andrew had a passion for bringing other people to Christ. On three occasions we find him doing this. On the first occasion, Andrew brought his own brother, Simon Peter, to meet the Master. With excitement in his voice, Andrew probably shouted his fantastic discovery, Peter, we have found the Messiah! (John 1:41). Meaning, I have the Messiah and you need to find Him too! It is a blessed moment of divine grace when a soul finds the Savior.

But it is further grace to be able to introduce others to Christ who are family members. That is grace upon grace, for not all family members are open to the gospel. Jesus said that this would be the case. The Lord warned that He would bring division to many homes. And so it has been the testimony of time.

There are heartbreaking situations where children reject the Lord of the parents, and defy both God and man. There are homes where the children come to faith, but are suppressed in expressing their love for the Lord by attending Sunday and Church because a parent will not let them go. There are other situations where a husband is antagonistic to the wife because of her new found faith. Or, a wife is jealous of the new religious fervor of her husband. A spiritual sword has split the family.

And yet, it is still worth every effort to tell family members about the Messiah, as Andrew told his brother, Peter. The best missionary field is still one's own family. As Andrew brought an adult, Simon, to the Lord for salvation, so he brought a child to Christ for spiritual service. It was Andrew who found a little boy who had five loaves and two fishes to help feed a hungry crowd (John 6:8–9).

In context, Jesus had been preaching to a gathering of 5,000 people. Suppertime had come and the people were hungry. Calling one of His disciples named Philip aside, the Lord said unto him, Philip, where shall we buy bread, which these may eat? Buy bread for 5,000 people for one meal? Lord, have you talked to Judas lately? The purse is almost empty Lord. Philip did some fast thinking and finally gave his analysis. Lord, 200 days' worth of the wages of a laboring man would not buy enough bread for all these people even if everyone ate just a little (John 6:7). At this point, Andrew, who overheard the initial question, had also been doing some thinking and some searching. If there was not enough money to buy food, maybe some of the people brought some food with them and the people could share. It was not a bad thought. It was a very practical thought. Andrew made a frantic search of the crowd, but all he could come up with was a lad with five rolls and two small fish. The eye of faith had spotted someone who could possibly be of use to Jesus, but it was the voice of doubt that prevailed. What are they among so many (John 6:9)?

In matchless grace, Jesus ignored the voice of doubt and honored the faith expressed, for the lad that Andrew introduced was used in a wonderful way that day, and the lesson is learned. We never know whom the Lord might use for His honor and glory. He might even use a little child. If ever there is a reason to bring children to Christ, here it is. From childish resources the Lord performed one of His greatest miracles. For those who work with the young people, here is great hope. Is a Sunday school program worth all the effort? Is a Vacation Bible School program worth the effort? Is a youth program worth the effort? Andrew would say, Yes! He once introduced a child to Christ and amazing things happened. As far as Andrew's work? Well, God honors those who honor Him. The faith may be weak, but the motive can be pure, and if pure, it is priceless.

There is a third time we find Andrew in the Bible, and once more he is found introducing someone to Christ (John 12:20–22). As the next situation unfolds, some Greeks had come to Philip with a request to see Jesus. Philip did not really know what to do with these Jewish proselytes, so he asked Andrew. Without hesitation, Andrew knew what to do. He brought the Greeks to Jesus. Andrew understood enough about the Lord to realize that

He was never too busy to give of Himself to earnest and sincere searchers for the truth. Andrew understood also that the heart of Christ was large enough to love Gentiles as well as Jews.

So here we have the biblical record of an apostle who had a consuming passion for the eternal, the practical, and the spiritual welfare of people. Such soul winning and soul caring concern is commendable and worthy of imitation. May God help us to be soul-winners for the Savior in a day and age that has grown careless over souls. Wyn and Charles Arn have written about this sad situation in their book, *The Master's Plan for Discipleship*. On pages 7–11, they give several characteristics of American Christianity, three of which are disturbing.

Reaching non-Christians is a low priority for most congregations and individuals. Most Christians routinely ignore what was the main priority of the believers in the book of Acts – reaching others for Christ.

The biblical concept of souls being "lost" has disappeared from the conscience of most churches and most Christians. We need a fresh awareness that people who die without Christ will spend an eternity in hell. Hell is not only a doctrine, it is a reality. Evangelism is much discussed, but little practiced. Others are not won to Christ, in part, because the purpose of salvation is often forgotten. Every Christian has been invited to be fishers of men. All of us need to be more like Andrew.

> Speak for the love of God,
>   And speak for the love of man;
> For the words of truth love sends abroad
>   Can never be in vain.

Now there is something else we must see. Not only is what Andrew did commendable, he brought others to Christ, but the way he worked is also special. Andrew was rather low-keyed in his approach. Andrew was not like Peter, nor like James or John, who burned with religious fervor. These men of intense emotion could not wait to engage in religious activity, and rightly so.

They had found the Messiah. They had found the truth. They had found the kingdom of heaven. They had found the solution to all the problems of life. They had found the Savior.

Peter, James, and John could hardly contain themselves when it came to religious zeal for the Lord. And God needs such men and women in His service, for they do stir others up to think and to work. But there is also a place for the Andrews. The Andrews of the Kingdom might be overshadowed by others with more knowledge, more zeal, more presence, and more personality, but they are often the ones who have led the leaders to the Lord.

The world knows the name of Billy Graham, but how many have ever heard of Mordicia Ham, the evangelist that led Billy Graham to Christ when he was about 17 years old? The world knows the name of D. L. Moody, but how many know about the faithful Boston Sunday school teacher who determined on April 21, 1855 to go to the young shoe clerk working at Holton's Shoe Store and not leave until the gospel had been shared? His name? Edward Kimball. There is a place for humble servants who are faithful soul winners for the Savior.

I do not think that Andrew ever really cared who got the glory as long as the Lord overshadowed him. But that is a hard lesson to learn. Little slights are often taken far too seriously, and raw emotion erupts over wounded pride. It is understandable; it is also wrong. The principle is still true: if Jesus Christ is glorified, and His work is advanced, then it does not matter who gets the credit. Perhaps Andrew was even proud of his brother Peter when Simon stood to speak on the Day of Pentecost and 3,000 souls were saved.

Outside of two brief cameo appearances, the biblical narrative is silent about Andrew. Andrew was part of the group of four disciples that asked Jesus three questions leading up to the Olivet Discourse (cf. Mark 13:3–4) and he was present in prayer on the Day of Pentecost (Acts 1:13–14). Only church tradition offers an ending to his labors of love for the Lord. Andrew has the distinction of being the patron saint of three countries: Russia, Greece, and Scotland. The implication is that he traveled widely preaching the gospel until his death. The only certain thing is that Andrew was faithful unto death.

Appealing once more to tradition, it was in the town of Patros, in Greece, that Andrew died a martyr's death. Having been arrested by Aegeas, the governor of the area, Andrew was put in prison. Aegeas was hostile to Christians after his wife Maximilla was converted to Christ. In his rage to punish a Christian, seven soldiers whipped Andrew. He was then taken and bound to an X-shaped cross instead of nailed to it. The intent was to prolong the suffering. The followers of Andrew recorded that as he approached the cross he embraced the ordeal calmly, saying: I have long desired and expected this happy hour. The cross has been consecrated by the body of Christ hanging on it. For two days, as long as strength remained, Andrew preached Christ to his tormentors. In this manner he entered into heaven to receive the Crown of Life in the year of our Lord, A.D. 69. In summary, one author notes, Andrew sought for souls selflessly, he sought people out optimistically, and he sought for souls universally. These are enduring qualities for all Christians to strive to possess.

5

Philip: A Faithful Follower

There are many surprises to be found in the Bible, one of which is how little the New Testament speaks of the major figures of the early church. Philip offers a primary example. Though an apostle of the Lord Jesus Christ, Philip is rescued from historical obscurity by the Gospel of John. What is recorded is not much, but it is instructive. The Bible says that Philip came from Bethsaida in Galilee, which is the same town from which Peter and Andrew came (John 1:44). Perhaps they knew each other as children, and worked as adults in the same trade. It is possible that Philip was a fisherman, though that is uncertain. What is certain is that it was to Philip that Jesus spoke the compelling words calling him to discipleship. Jesus said simply enough, Follow me (John 1:43)! Lord, where are you going? Follow me and see! Lord, will it be fun? Will it be easy to follow you? No, not always. That is why you must count the cost. There are three reasons why it is not easy to follow Christ.

First, to follow Christ means to stop following the ways of the world. Society does not like the new standards of living demanded by Christ. New attitudes and new responses are called for in practicing Christians, as the Sermon on the Mount indicates (Matt. 5:1—7:29; note 5:43–48). If the world finds pleasure in the philosophy and practice of hedonism, the Christian must not. And it is those differences which challenges and convicts the world of sin, righteousness, and judgment to come. To follow Christ means to stop following the ways of the world.

Second, to follow Christ means to be at war with the Devil. In Revelation 13:7, we read of the Beast. And it was given unto him to make war with the saints. Satan does not give up his children easily to the Kingdom of God. He has many ways to hold them hostage to sin. Many years ago the Puritan preacher, Thomas Brooks wrote a famous work with the title, *Precious Remedies Against Satan's Devices*. Rev. Brooks wanted to arm the people of God against satanic trickery. He observed several of the ways that the Evil One tries to deceive the elect into sinning.

Satan presents sin with virtuous colors. More than one person has justified their behavior in questionable situations by insisting that the moment defines true ethics, not some arbitrary objective standard. In 1986, before a senatorial worldwide television audience, a former Marine officer named Oliver North proudly declared that he would trade lives for lies in order to justifying engaging in an illegal covert operation. The colors of virtue were flown high without any qualifications or recognition that sometimes the lesser of two evils must be chosen. Rahab the harlot offers one example, as per Hebrews 11:31.

Satan suggests that sin is not offensive to God. The essence of God is viewed as being all of mercy. While God delights to show mercy, He is also a holy God who hates sin and will not let the guilty go free. There will be a payday, some day (cf. Rom. 14:11).

Satan encourages sin by teaching that repentance is easy. Superficial repentance is very easy, but genuine repentance is another work of divine grace for it works sorrow in the heart. The repentance of Peter, and the repentance of Judas, were quite different.

Satan promotes sin by taunting the soul to partake of the same activities that other individuals are openly doing. There is an unholy boldness in sin (Rom. 1:27–32).

Satan enhances the inclination to sin by reminding the heart of the outward mercies that others enjoy while they walk in the ways of evil. The Christian looks around and sees a multitude of individuals with money, power, and success, engaged in riotous laughter and behavior as if life were all a party (Psa. 73:16–18).

Satan offers comfort in sin by having people compare themselves with others who are more militant in outrageous behavior. The spirit of the Pharisee is present in every generation. There are many other devices of Satan, for he is a very clever personality, and very successful in the art of deceit, destruction, and the damnation of the soul.

Third, to follow Christ means to be in conflict with the darker side of self. The Apostle Paul wrote about the great internal struggle that takes place in the heart of the Christian (Rom. 7:14–25). To follow Christ means to engage in open conflict with the inner man. Despite all of the difficulties associated with discipleship, Philip was given the privilege of hearing Jesus saying, Follow me. Follow me and fight the world. Follow me and wage a noble warfare with the Wicked One. Follow me and declare open hostility on your corruption. If your right hand offends you, cut if off. If your right eye offends, pluck it out. Deal savagely and ruthless with inward corruption. And Philip said, I will follow you Lord, and I will fight the good fight of the faith.

As we watch Philip in the service of the Savior, we learn bits and pieces about him from his brief cameo appearances. We discover that Philip was missionary-minded. After Jesus called Philip to discipleship, the Bible says that he found his brother Nathaniel, and said unto him, We have found Him of whom Moses in the law and in the prophets did write, Jesus of Nazareth, the son of Joseph (John 1:45).

From a human perspective, that was true. What Philip would later learn, from a divine perspective, is that long before he ever found Christ, Jesus had searched him out with an eternal love (Rom. 8:28–32). You have not chosen me, Philip, said the Lord one day, but I have chosen you and ordained you (John 15:16). The difference is important to notice between man searching for God, and God revealing Himself, for the larger issue at stake is, Who will get the glory for the salvation of the soul?

The Bible teaches that salvation is of the Lord. Philip only found Jesus because the Lord had marked him out for special favor. Being predestinated to eternal life, Philip was effectually called to salvation, and to service. Such matchless grace should be humbling to all that come to faith. With religious zeal in his heart, Philip immediately invited Nathaniel to make the same discovery he had made, but Nathaniel was skeptical. "Can anything good come out of Nazareth," he asked with a cynical smile (John 1:46)"

As a town, Nazareth had a terrible reputation. For many today, it would be like asking, "Can anything good come out of Bourbon Street, New Orleans, Louisiana?" Philip shows tremendous wisdom in religious restraint. He did not begin a debate with Nathaniel concerning Christ. Philip had the weight of the Law and the Prophets on his side. Philip could have said many things, but he said simply enough, Come and see! Sometimes that is still the best way to witness. Debates are not at all profitable. To the person who questions the Church, or Christ, or Christianity, the best invitation is still, Come and see.

As Philip was practical in bringing souls to the Savior, he was a very practical man in other matters as well, reflected in the feeding of 5,000 men, plus women and children. The story is told in John 6. Jesus had been preaching to a large multitude. The hour grew late and the Lord decided He would have the people stay for something to eat. Turning to Philip, the Lord asked an astonishing question: Philip, where shall we buy bread that these people may eat?

The Lord had no intention of buying bread; He just wanted to test Philip's reaction to a potential crisis. Philip searched the sea of surging humanity spread out before him, made a quick calculation, and came to a definite conclusion: the situation was hopeless. There were too many people for the limited resources of the disciples. A year's pay would not buy enough bread to feed this crowd, even if everyone only ate a little (John 6:5–7). From a human perspective, Philip's assessment of the situation was accurate. The disciples did not have enough resources. The crowd was very large.

It would take a year's wages, and more, to feed everyone, even if everyone ate very little.

Philip is not selfish. He has a warm heart. He wants to feed the people. But what can the disciples do? The correct answer is, Nothing! The Disciples can do nothing on their own, which is the point the Lord wanted them to learn time and again. There are several occasions when Christ brought together circumstances beyond the control of the disciples in order to teach them one of the greatest of all spiritual lessons: without the Lord we can do nothing in life. We cannot live well, we cannot think well, we cannot love well, or lead well. We cannot work well, or win souls to the Savior, without Christ.

Without a doubt, as the Lord tested His first disciples, so He will test the rest. From time to time, the Lord will allow the pressures of life to mount against us in order that we might be totally dependent upon Him. We will find ourselves hopeless and helpless in a great and grave situation. This divine technique has been used time and again. It was used with Moses at the Red Sea. It was used with David against Saul. It was used with Joseph in the dungeon. The Lord knows how to humble His people so that they do not constantly rely upon their natural resources. The Lord knows how to focus the attention of His children upon Himself so that He receives honor and glory, while faith is increased.

Sometimes professing Christians fail the test of genuine faith. They turn back to the world, the flesh, and the devil (Matt. 13:1–9; 13:18–23). For some, if God does not help resolve a situation in a predetermined manner, then He does not care. But that is neither true nor fair. The faith of God's true children rises to the challenge. Faith triumphs, and cries with Job, "Though He slay me, yet will I trust Him" (Job 13:15). Philip was willing to trust the Lord.

We know this, for when Christ began to give instruction as to what should be done, Philip did his part in the preparations. Then he stepped aside to see what God in Christ might do , and the true Bread of Life fed the people from heaven (John 6:10–13).

As Philip looked and wondered at the performance of the mighty miracle, his faith grew, and a determination was made: whatever the situation, I will bring it to Jesus. Therefore, we are not surprised to discover that when a group of Greeks had come to Jerusalem wanting to visit, he found a way to bring them to Christ (John 12:20–22). That the Greeks should first approach Philip about Christ is not unusual. Perhaps the Greeks thought that they found in him a contact, for Philip is a Greek name meaning, Lover of horses. Though Philip was a Jew, he had a Greek name. A bit of speculation suggests how that came to pass. History records that about ten years before the birth of Christ, there was a local king in the province of Ituraea called Philip the Tetrarch. For political reasons he raised the status of Bethsaida, and made it the capitol of the province. Perhaps Philip the apostle was named in honor of the Tetrarch, who had done so much for the region in which he lived.

Regardless of his name, when the Greeks contacted Philip, he was ready to help them the best he could. He would bring them to Christ, but first, he wanted counsel, and so he told Andrew about the situation. Was this hesitancy of Philip in bringing the Greeks directly to the Lord indicative of a man who disliked responsibly, and so recoiled from important decisions forced upon him (John 12:20–22)? It has been suggested. While that may be a rather harsh judgment against Philip, there is something that can be learned: it is not wrong to have others help in making an important decision. When a person is aware of their own weaknesses, and seeks help, that is wisdom.

Philip had wisdom in the form of common sense, and he also had something else: a longing to know God intimately. This facet of Philip's faith is manifested in the Upper Room the night of the Last Supper with the Savior. Jesus was sharing how He would soon be going to the Father. Philip was confused, and said simply, Lord, shew us the Father, and it will sufficeth us. And Jesus responded to Philip by saying, He that hath seen me hath seen the Father (John 14:8–9). Here is the heart of Christianity: Jesus is God. The attributes and essences of God are the attributes and essence of Christ. To see Jesus is to see God. If we want to know God the Father, all we have to do is to look at God the Son. It is as simple, and profound, as that.

While there is nothing more said about Philip in the New Testament, many fantastic legends arose about him in the early church. According to one story, Philip went to Athens where three hundred philosophers gathered to meet him. The Athenians were always interested in hearing something new. After the gospel was preached, the philosophers asked for three days to think things over. In the discussion that followed, it was decided that an appeal should be made to the Jewish high priest at Jerusalem for clarification about Christ.

When Ananias the high priest heard that Jesus was being preached, he led a force of five hundred men to destroy Philip. Philip smote them all with blindness, and then ordered the earth to open and consume Ananias to the knees. Rather than repent, Ananias pronounced everything as witchcraft. So Philip ordered the earth to take Ananias up to the waist. Still Ananias was not repentant, and so the earth swallowed him up to the neck.

And still Ananias refused to yield the point. Finally, Philip ordered the earth to consume Ananias completely, which it did. His high priestly robe flew away where it has not been found to this day. It is an interesting story, though it never happened. Philip's moral life came to an end at Hierapolis at the age of 87. By ministering in Lydia, Parthia, and Gaul, he was one of the great spiritual leaders of Asia.[6]

Before he died by cruel scourging and crucifixion (c. A.D. 52), according to legend Philip made an unusual request that his body should be wrapped, not in linen, but in papyrus, for he was not worthy that even his dead body should be handled in the same manner as the Lord's. And they buried him as he directed. And a heavenly voice said that he had received the crown of life. In the sixth century, Pope John III (A.D. 560–572) acquired the body of Philip from Hieropolis and re-interned it in a church in Rome. Today, so it is said, a traveler can see the large marble sarcophagus where the bones of the apostle Philip rest. In the end, Philip was faithful unto death. The life Philip lived, and the death he died, should serve to encourage all believers to be a faithful follower of Christ.

---

[6] See Eusebius, *The Ecclesiastical History*, 3.21.

Doctrine of the World

1. The term *world* is used in Scripture in various ways.

    - It has reference to the geographical earth (Job 34:13).
    - It has reference to the various nations on the earth (Matt. 28:19–20).
    - It has reference to the material goods of this earth (Matt. 16:26).
    - It has reference to the normal inhabitants on the earth (Psa. 9:8).
    - It has reference to a certain portion of the people (Luke 2:1).
    - It has reference to the unregenerate that oppose Christ (Matt. 18:7).
    - It has reference to the prevailing philosophy of the unregenerate (1 John 2:15).
    - It has reference to a future new order of nature (Matt. 5:32; Luke 18:30).

2. Christians are considered by Christ to be the true light of the world, or the guiding influence in the moral darkness into which sin has brought all things (Matt. 5:14).

3. The cares, or interests of this world, can destroy any spiritual sensitivity of the soul (Matt. 13:22).

4. If a person owned everything in the world and yet lost his soul, the material possession would be of no avail (Matt. 16:26; Luke 9:25).

5. Jesus pronounced a judgment upon the world of His day (Matt. 18:7).

6. The gospel is to be preached in the entire world (Matt. 28:20).

7. The world had a beginning, and it shall have an end, as it is now known (Gen. 1:1; Matt. 25:34).

8. When Christ came into the world, people did not know Him as Creator and Lord (John 1:10).

9. Jesus came to take away the sin of the world (John 1:29; John 4:42).

10. Christ came into the world because of the love of God the Father (John 3:16).

11. Christ did not come the first time to condemn the world, but to save it (John 3:17; 12:47).

12. Christ is the True Light that has come into the world (John 3:19; 8:12; 9:5).

13. Jesus cast out the prince of this world (John 12:31) having judged him (John 16:11, 33).

14. The world will hate Christians, as they have hated Christ (John 15:18–19).

15. While they are in the world, Christians shall have many troubles (John 16:33) because they are not like the world (John 17:16).

16. Christians are the elect, chosen out of the world, to be conformed into the image of Christ (15:19).

17. The power of the gospel turned the world of the Jews and Gentiles upside down (Acts 17:6).

18. Everyone in the world is guilty before God of transgressing His law (Rom. 3:19; 4:13; 5:12–13).

19. The Christians, having been redeemed, must not be conformed, or pressed into the mold of this world any longer (Rom. 12:1–2).

20. The gospel makes the wisdom of this world appear foolish (1 Cor. 1:20).

21. Christians are mocked by the world (1 Cor. 4:9).

22. Christians are to be crucified to the world (Gal. 6:14) so that they do not love it (1 John 2:15). If anyone loves the world, the love of the Father is not present in his heart.

23. There are demons of darkness which rule over a spiritual part of the unregenerate world's system (Eph. 6:12).

24. Since men bring nothing into this world, they can take nothing out (1 Tim. 6:7).

25. The world is hostile to God (Jas. 4:4).

26. Those who are born of God are destined to overcome the world (1 John 5:4).

27. Though the present world lies in the Evil One (1 John 5:19), one day the kingdoms of this world shall become the kingdom of God (Rev. 11:15).

$$6$$

Bartholomew: A Sermon from Silence

I n the list of the apostles found in Mark (3:16–19), Matthew (10:2–4), Luke (6:14–16), and Acts (1:13), the name of Bartholomew appears. However, there is no further reference to him in the New Testament. While it is characteristic of the Scriptures to emphasize the message and not the man, it seems extraordinary that no information be given about one of the pillars of the Church. Perhaps there is a solution to the concern. Sometime in the ninth century A.D., a man named Elias, of Damascus, set forth the proposition that Bartholomew could be identified with Nathanael (John 1:45–51). Since then, many reputable scholars have agreed, and contend that Bartholomew is Nathanael, for the following reasons.

Bartholomew is not a first name, but a distinguishing second name. The word *Bar*, means "son of." Perhaps the apostle was Nathanael Bartholomew, or Nathanael, the son of Tolmai (cf. 2 Sam. 13:37).

The first three Gospels—Matthew, Mark, and Luke—never mention Nathanael, while John's Gospel never mentions Bartholomew. When Nathanael is mentioned in the fourth Gospel, he is spoken of in such a way that he is an apostle (John 1:43–51; cf. John 21:2). Nathanael was with Peter, James, John, and Thomas when they met with the Master following His resurrection.

In the lists of the Twelve, the names of Philip and Bartholomew always occur together, as if it were natural to speak of them in such a manner. It was Philip who brought Nathanael to Christ.

If Bartholomew is Nathanael, then the total silence of Scripture is broken, and we learn something about the man, beginning with his friendship with Philip. Most people meet many others in life who are very special, but true friendship is rare. It is tested in fires of disappointment and disagreement. It is also manifested in whether or not someone has the best interest of the other person in mind. Philip had the best interest of Nathanael in his heart, for he tried to bring him to Christ. Because you truly care for someone, bring them to Christ.

When Philip informed Nathanael of his own great discovery (John 1:45), he was skeptical, and asked, Can there any good thing come out of Nazareth? It was not pride or prejudice that prompted this immediate response, but a deep sense of personal shame. Nathanael was also a Galilean, and as such, felt the social stigma of his day. Nathanael knew all too well how the people of Judea felt toward Galileans, and so he wondered if the Messiah could really come from among the poor and obscure part of Palestine.

Had Nathanael known the Scriptures better, he might have realized that it was prophesied that Jesus would be as a root out of a dry ground (Isa. 53:2). It was foretold the Suffering Savior would have no physical beauty that people should desire Him (Isa. 53:3).

He would be despised and rejected of men, a man of sorrows and acquainted with grief (Isa. 53:3). Can any good thing come out of Nazareth? asked Nathanael. Come and see, said Philip (John 1:46).

Nathanael came to Christ, and was shocked to see the Lord in His splendor and glory, for immediately Nathanael learned something about Jesus: He was all knowing. As soon as Jesus saw Nathanael, He said three things about him.

First, the Lord commended his faith. Behold, an Israelite indeed! What did Christ mean? He meant that in Nathanael there was genuine faith, for, "Not all Israel is Israel." According to Scripture, the true Israelite is the person who has the faith of Abraham, Isaac, and Jacob. A true Israelite is a person who is seriously religious.

To draw a modern day parallel, it could be said of someone in this generation, There is a Christian, who is a Christian indeed. The meaning would be clear. There are those who take the Christian life seriously:

- The Bible is read and meditated upon.
- A local church is identified with and supported with spiritual gifts.
- Missionaries are supported.
- There is gospel obedience to the ordinance of baptism.
- The hour of worship is longed for.
- Christ is loved and God is worshipped in spirit and in truth.
- Souls are sought out for salvation.

- The Scriptures are diligently studied.
- A life of prayer is found to be pleasant and profitable.

There are Christians indeed, and there were Israelites, indeed.

Second, Jesus commended Nathanael for his virtue. Nathanael was not only religious, but he was righteous. He was a child of grace, and part of the covenant blessings. He was fortunate to have escaped the pollution of this world with vices that haunt the heart and destroy the happiness of the soul. He was not a weak man who wanted to love virtue, but found himself enslaved to some sin. He was good, and decent, and upright, but he still needed salvation, because good works can never justify a person in the sight of God. Virtue can be commended, but it does not save.

Then, *third,* the Lord commended Nathanael for his transparency. Behold an Israelite indeed, in whom is no guile [or deceit]. There was no subtlety in Nathanael like there was in other men such as the patriarch Jacob. Jacob tricked his father, Isaac, and stole the family blessing by deceit. Nathanael was as clear as crystal in his conscience, and that was reflected in his countenance. David, king of Israel, described the guileless man in Psalm 15.

> Lord, who shall abide in thy tabernacle?
>> Who shall dwell in thy holy hill?
> He that walketh uprightly, and worketh
>> Righteousness, and speaketh the truth in his heart.
> He that backbiteth not with his tongue,
>> Nor doeth evil to his neighbor,
> Nor taketh up a reproach against his neighbor.

When Nathanael heard the assessment of Christ upon his life, he was astonished, and responded to the flattery with amazement. How do you know me? He asked, and learned something about the deity of Christ. The Lord knows what is in all men, just like He knows what is in your heart and mine. The Lord knows who you are, and what you really want in life, but also what you are doing every moment of every hour of the day. Nathanael, said Christ, I saw you when you were under the fig tree.

The fig tree is used in Scripture symbolically to refer to Israel as a nation (Matt. 24:32), because under the fig tree pious Jews would go to pray and meditate. Under the shade of the tree Nathanael thought no one would notice if he communed with God, but under the fig tree the King in His beauty saw Nathanael. Has the Lord ever seen you under the fig tree? Do you have a shady place of spiritual rest where you go to be with God? Do you have a sacred spot somewhere to pray and meditate with the King of Glory? William Law, in his book, *A Serious Call to a Devout and Holy Life*, offers this counsel: Pray always in the same place: reserve that place for devotion, and never allow yourself to do anything common in it.

Adam and Eve once had a shady place in Paradise, where, in the cool of each evening, they walked with the Lord.

Isaac had a shady place in the green field at even tide.

Elijah had a special place in the mountain cave.

Jesus had a special place in the Garden of Gethsemane.

As Jesus spoke, the heart of Nathanael opened up, and he made a great confession manifesting a converted heart, as he said, Rabbi, thou art the Son of God; thou art the king of Israel. And

Jesus smiled. Nathanael, do you now believe? I know you believe, and because of that, I will show you greater things. Faith is always rewarded with more faith. Nathanael, hereafter, you shall see the heavens open, and the angels of God, ascending and descending upon the Son of God. Now follow me (John 1:51).

With Philip, Nathanael followed Christ, and so was present when the omnipotent power of Christ was manifested following the Lord's resurrection. The story is told in John 21. In a final meal, Jesus fed His faithful disciples from His own abundant resources, and they were satisfied (John 21:6). And so we have two cameo appearances of Nathanael. At the beginning of the Lord's ministry he was a witness to omniscience and omnipresence. At the end of the Lord's ministry he was an eyewitness to His omnipotence. These things become compelling reasons for many to accept the proposition that Nathanael is Bartholomew, and one of the Twelve Apostles. However, to be honest, biblical scholars are not united in this matter. The *Encyclopedia of Religion* notes that ". . . identification with Nathanael in John 1:45 is only conjectural." Here are the logical concerns of identifying Nathanael as Bartholomew.

It was 800 years before Christians made a linkage between Nathanael and Bartholomew, which leads to a word of warning. New ideals and insights into the Scriptures unheard of by previous generations should always be suspect. That is how error is born and breeds heresy.

A basic principle of Biblical study is to speak when the Scriptures speak, and to be silent when the Scriptures are silent. Novel interpretations of the Bible are enjoyable, and interesting, but usually unprofitable to the soul.

If God the Holy Spirit wanted to say more about Bartholomew, He would have done so. The man, as well as his message, would have been made plainer. And yet, there is a sermon from silence. There are practical lessons to be learned.

In the kingdom of God, the first shall be last, and the last shall be first. Today, the apostles are honored. Special holy days are set aside as their names adorn religious structures throughout the world. The last is now first. And yet, the silence that initially surrounded Bartholomew testifies that he did not mind being obscure if Jesus Christ was exalted. He was not out to make a name for himself in the world of religion; he only wanted to preach Christ.

Those who are worthy of honor can be dishonored by unworthy deeds committed in their name. Perhaps you have heard of the St. Bartholomew Massacre. It is a matter of history that on August 24, 1572, the Catholic Church began a great massacre of Huguenots, in France, on St. Bartholomew's Day. The Huguenots were French Calvinist Protestants. More than 30,000 men, women, and children were killed without mercy with the approval of King Charles IX under the influence of his mother, Catherine de Medici.

In the kingdom of God there are many unsung heroes of the faith: countless Sunday school teachers, pastors of small churches, missionaries on foreign fields, and shut-ins, that will never be recognized in this world. There are many gifted people who go unloved, un-rewarded, and unwanted by the world. Hebrews 11 speaks of nameless saints who "had trials of cruel mockings and scourgings, yea moreover of bonds and imprisonment: they were stoned, they were sawn asunder, were tempted, were slain with the sword; they wandered about in sheepskin and goatskins; being destitute, afflicted, tormented; of whom the world was not worthy." Bartholomew represents all the silent souls who are unknown to men, but who are well known to God.

In the final analysis, to have one's name on the roll of the Book of Life is reward enough. In Revelation 20, a terrifying scene is witnessed. John sees all of the dead standing before the final judgment of Christ. There is a Great White Throne, and on the throne sits the Son of God. He lifts up His eyes and beholds millions upon countless souls, for all of humanity stands before Him. The face of each person is intent upon the throne. An angel flies overheard. He is carrying a large scroll. With majestic solemnity, the angel hands the scroll to the Lord. Slowly the scroll is unrolled. Ears strain as individual names are called. By each name there is the record of human deeds. And they were judged every man according to their own works. "And whosoever was not written in the Book of Life was cast into the Lake of Fire" (v. 15).

It is not wrong for each person to ask, Is my name written in the Book of Life? Does heaven have a record of my holy works? While salvation is by grace, through faith apart from works, we will be judged for the deeds done in our body, both good and evil. Jesus told the Apostles, rejoice because your names are written in heaven (Luke 10:20). Bartholomew's name was written in the Book of Life. It is enough.

Despite the absence of concrete information about Bartholomew in the biblical narrative, there are some obvious things, which can be noted.

Bartholomew was a privileged man. In the providence of God, Bartholomew was numbered among the chosen twelve to be a pillar of the New Testament church. The Lord God is sovereign. He has a right to make and create whom He wills, and how He wills. Every individual exists at the good pleasure of His will. We are appointed our appropriate place in the Divine decree of things. Bartholomew's place was as an apostle.

Not only was Bartholomew a privileged man because of his place in the kingdom of heaven, but he was privileged because of what he was a witness to. Bartholomew was present when Jesus preached a sermon to a large crowd gathered on a mountainside. He was standing nearby when Jesus touched the blind, and made people see, spoke to the cripple and made them walk. He watched in awe when Jesus spoke at a funeral, and the dead lived. Bartholomew sat at the table of the Lord's Last Supper. He touched Jesus, prayed with Him, and learned the great lessons of life. The mercy of God fell greatly upon Bartholomew, and he did not prove to be unworthy of the Divine mercies.

Bartholomew was faithful unto death. As we turn to the legends that surround the name of Bartholomew, care is taken for many fantastic things are claimed about each of the apostles. There are three places Bartholomew is alleged to have ministered.

He is said to have ministered in India. The early church historians, Eusebius and Jerome, record a story associated with Bartholomew in India (Eusebius, *The Ecclesiastical History*, 5.10.3;

Jerome, *Concerning Illustrious Men*, 36). There was a well-known stoic philosopher of Alexandria named Pantaenus, who came to faith in Christ and went to preach in India. When he arrived, he was amazed to discover many converts. For Bartholomew, one of the apostles, had preached to them, and left them with the writing of Matthew in the Hebrew language, which they would have preserved till that time.

He is said to have ministered in Phyrgia. And here he was killed, despite the stories that he escaped martyrdom, and lived to preach the gospel elsewhere.

He is said to have ministered in Armenia. The Armenian Church claims Bartholomew as its founder. Here Bartholomew is said to have preached with great power. A personal description of him is given. He has black curly hair, white skin, large eyes, straight nose, his hair covers his ears, his beard long and grizzled, and average height. He wears a white robe with a purple stripe, and a white cloak with four purple gems at the corners. For twenty-six years he has worn these, and they never grow old. His shoes have lasted twenty-six years. He prays a hundred times a day and a hundred times a night. His voice is like a trumpet; angels wait upon him; he is always cheerful, and knows all languages.

The legends and the physical descriptions are all very interesting, and so is the apocryphal Gospel of Bartholomew. This spurious writing describes a series of questions that Bartholomew addressed to Jesus and to Mary in the time between the resurrection and the ascension.

First, Bartholomew asked Jesus where He went from the Cross. The Lord answered that He went down from the Cross to

Hades, and brought forth thence all the patriarchs and came again unto the Cross.

Second, Bartholomew asked how many souls die, and are born each day. The answer is that 30,000 souls die each day, of whom only 3,000 are found righteous; and 30,001 souls are born each day into the world.

Third, Bartholomew asked Mary about the Annunciation, and Mary described her experience in great detail. The summary of the life of Bartholomew is simple since the New Testament reveals nothing about him except his name. The legends that arose around him are valuable, for they reveal a man who intimately knew the Lord, and lived to introduce others to Him.

According to tradition, Bartholomew died a painful death. He was first flayed alive for his preaching in Armenia, and then he was punctured through the thighs with a spear after being severely beaten by clubs. If that is true, then the church is reminded once more that it is blessed with a rich spiritual heritage of self-sacrificing, suffering souls. Surely the apostles are worthy of our admiration, and even our gratitude. In the person of Bartholomew, we are reminded that we are a privileged people. Millions have lived and died without hearing the gospel, or the name of Jesus. We have. And for those who desire to know Christ intimately, we are even more privileged, for Christ said that anyone, who came to Him, He would never cast out.

Finally, in the person of Bartholomew, we discover a sense of unworthiness in ourselves. All of the apostles, with one exception, entered into the sufferings of the Lord in a very real way. They were all faithful men unto death. And so the songwriter asks,

Must Jesus bear the Cross alone,
    And all the world go free?
No! there's a cross for everyone,
    And there's a cross for me.

Bartholomew is the quiet man among the apostles. He does not speak in Scripture officially, but I think I hear him saying, My life with Christ was worth it all. And to that end we can all say, Amen.

7

Matthew: Transforming the Treasures of Time

"And as Jesus passed forth from thence, he saw a man, named Matthew, sitting at the receipt of custom: and he saith unto him, Follow me. And he arose, and followed him" (Matt. 9:9).

The general facts surrounding the man named Matthew can be easily summarized since very little is known about him.

Matthew was the brother of James the Less, and the son of Alphaeus and Mary (Mark 2:14). It is interesting to note the three sets of brothers that are listed in the first twelve disciples. There is James and John, Peter and Andrew, and now Matthew and James the Less. It is a special measure of God's grace when family members come to faith.

Matthew was sometimes called Levi (lit. joined), which spoke of his family heritage. Matthew was from the tribe of Levi. The tribe of Levi had been set apart in a special way to conduct the worship of the Lord (Num. 3:6; Deut. 10:8). When the Law of Moses was given, the Levites were instructed to join with the sons of Aaron in spiritual service (cf. Num. 18:1–2). The centuries passed and this arrangement worked out fine. Generations came and went. Young people were instructed in the duties of the Temple, like Matthew. Beginning in childhood, Matthew would have been trained for the day he would enter into the holy work. But his heart wandered from the ways of God. He became hardened to the point that he could engage the enemies of Israel for money. He disgraced his family and his heritage. For a period of time, Matthew did not care what pain and grief he caused his parents, or what society thought of him. He would work for Rome.

Having become a moral reproach to the Levitical priesthood, Matthew decided to be numbered among those responsible for the security of Roman revenue as a custom's officer in Capernaum, in the territory ruled by Herod Antipas. The popular title for this position was *publicani*, from the Latin *publicanus*, because of the close relation to the public purse. As a publican, Matthew was in a position to become very wealthy.

Being a custom's official was financially a very profitable occupation (cf. Luke 19:8; Luke 3:12, 18), but there was a heavy emotional and mental price to pay. Of all the types of people in the ancient world, the tax collectors were hated above all others. The Jews excelled all others in their hatred for publicans. For Matthew to be a tax collector was for him to be a traitor to his own country. Rome enslaved the people of Palestine. To work for Rome was to be disloyal to one's nation. That was bad enough. But there was something else.

The Jews were convinced that they should only pay taxes to God. For an orthodox Jew, Yahweh was the only person to whom it was right to pay tribute, and that was done through the local synagogue. Since Matthew did not work as a priest in the Temple, he was violating religious honor due to God. No wonder the Jews numbered the publicans among the murderers and robbers of society.

A common proverb of the day instructed the young men to, Take not a wife out of that family wherein is a publican, for they are all publicans, or thieves, robbers, and wicked sinners.

Of course, Christ was aware of the intense social prejudice against publicans as a class of people. In one of His parables, the Lord spoke of a publican or tax collector, that stood afar off from the Temple (Luke 18:18). The publican stood far from the Temple in humility, and he stood far away from the House of God because he was not allowed by polite society to worship in the Temple. And that reminds us that it is possible to put unnecessary religious barriers before individuals who are struggling to find their way back to the Church.

Now there was some justification for the popular hostility of the Jews toward the tax collectors. They were notoriously greedy and unjust. It is a simple fact that individuals do grow bold in sin. And the bolder the sin, the bolder the person becomes in bad behavior. Because they were hard-hearted, the tax collectors invented a number of ways to extract money.

There was a production tax. One-tenth of a person's crop of grain, and one-fifth of his wine, fruit, and oil went to the government.

There was an income tax. One percent of a man's income was taken.

There was a poll tax. Everyone had to pay a portion of their income simply for the privilege of being alive. Men aged fourteen through sixty-five were taxed, and women twelve through sixty-five were taxed. One denarius, or one day's wage was the normal price extracted.

There was an import and an export tax.

There was a purchase tax on everything that was bought and sold.

For poor people politically enslaved and economically challenged, all the various taxes amounted to a heavy burden. But Matthew did not care. He was ruthless enough to join in the collection of money from his own people. Then one day, in the providence of God, the Holy Spirit was sent to work on Matthew's hard heart, and to bring conviction to his conscience. Matthew was ready to change, because money no longer satisfied him. There is a limit to what money can buy.

Money had not bought Matthew any friends or love. The only people he could associate with were fellow publicans, and the local prostitutes. But, even then, Matthew never knew if others liked him, or his wealth. In his autobiography, oil tycoon J. Paul Getty spoke of his five marriages, and wrote that he would give his considerable wealth for the true love of one woman.

Money had not brought Matthew a good conscience. While the heart of a person can become so callused that the misery of another is no longer seen or felt, there is a persistent thought that all is not right. There must be more to life than listening to people mutter under their breath, swindler, cheat, traitor, wicked man, crook. Because people have a moral standard of right and wrong, sometimes, with the aid of divine grace, they are ready to judge bad behavior even in themselves. Charles Wesley wrote:

> I want a principle within,
> Of jealous, godly fear;
> A sensibility of sin—
> A pain to feel it near:
>
> I want the first approach to feel
> Of pride, or fond desire;
> To catch the wandering of my will,
> And quench the kindling fire.
>
> From Thee that I no more may part,
> No more Thy goodness grieve,
> The filial awe, the fleshly heart,
> The tender conscience, give.
>
> Quick as the apple of an eye,
> O God, my conscience make;
> Awake my soul when sin is nigh,
> And keep it still awake.

Money had not bought Matthew a place in the kingdom of heaven. There is only one way to enter into the kingdom, and that is through the act of repentance. Repentance means to turn away from sin and self to the Savior. Repentance means to forsake the world as to its philosophy, its security, and its promises, in order to follow Christ. Matthew was a man who repented.

It happened one day while he was still sitting at the receipt of custom at Capernaum on the Great West Trunk Road from Damascus and the Far East to the Mediterranean Sea. Matthew looked up from his busy task of taking in money from the many travelers to observe the excitement of a crowd. In the middle of the multitude was a special Man. Matthew saw Him, and knew who He was. By now the word had spread throughout Palestine. Far and wide people had heard about the Carpenter from Galilee who claimed to be the Son of God. His name was Jesus. Some said He was the Messiah. Others thought that He was a prophet like Jeremiah.

Suddenly, Jesus started to move towards Matthew. In front of the booth the Lord of Glory stopped, and quietly stared down. Into Matthew's eyes the Lord looked, and beyond that His gaze penetrated Matthew's heart. While others saw a publican, a traitor, a scoundrel, and an extortionist, Jesus saw a sad soul in need of a Savior. Jesus saw a person ready to be rescued from the emptiness of pursuing the tarnished treasures of time.

Jesus saw a man who needed a friend. As the Friend of Sinners, Christ spoke to Matthew and said simply enough, Follow Me. Two words, and a man was moved. Two words, and a heart was changed. Two words, and a soul was rescued from the Kingdom of Darkness and was transformed into the Kingdom of Light. Two words, and a sinner was made into a saint.

Christ came to a man in the midst of sinful activity, and said, Follow me. Stop what you are doing, rise up, and follow Me. While some in the crowd gasped, the angels in heaven exploded in triumphant praise. Somewhere else in the celestial

City of God the redeemed of the ages rejoiced. From one end of heaven to the other the news went forth that a new name had been written down in the Lamb's Book of Life. Abraham! Isaac! Jacob! Come here. You sons of Aaron come here! Matthew has been saved. Matthew the Levite has come to faith. Matthew has repented. Matthew is willing to renounce his whole way of life. Jesus said, Follow me, and Matthew arose and followed Him. In the act of rising up to follow Christ, Matthew manifested that he was truly converted in several ways.

Matthew suddenly wanted others to come to Christ. Matthew wanted others to meet the Master. Therefore, on the night of the day of his salvation, Matthew held a dinner party to celebrate. Because Jesus was the Guest of Honor, many publicans and sinners came and sat down with him and His disciples (Matt. 9:20). In this way, Matthew began to witness to others that the most wretched and vile of men can know something about redeeming grace. May God grant us a longing to see souls saved. It is a sign of salvation.

Another sign of salvation is being the target of slander and scorn for righteousness sake. When the Pharisees heard of the dinner party Matthew held for the Lord, they became very critical. Approaching some of the original disciples, the Pharisees demanded to know why the Lord would eat with tax collectors, and others of ill repute. The disciples did not know what to say so they asked Christ, who knew just how to respond. Jesus pointed out something very simple. They that be whole need not a physician, but they that are sick. I am not come to call the righteous but sinners to repentance (Matt. 9:12–13).

Matthew knew he was a sinner. He had hurt many people. Nothing would ever change that fact. Matthew had lived a life of rebellion by defying His God, denouncing His country, and showing disrespect to his spiritual heritage. Matthew's passion had been inordinate for materialistic objects. But that was in the past. He was a repentant sinner, saved by grace.

As a saved sinner, as a Christian, Matthew manifested modesty. Humility touched his life, reflected in the fact that his name is not mentioned in his own gospel in any way that would call undue attention to himself. This facet of Matthew's character is worthy of emulation, for humility does not come easy to anyone. Perhaps one of the best definitions of humility has been given by Charles Fox, who wrote that humility is the willingness to be

> Foolish enough to depend on Christ for wisdom,
> Weak enough to be empowered with His strength,
> Base enough to have no honor but God's honor,
> Despised enough to be kept in the dust at His feet,
> Nothing enough for God to be everything.

It was a blessed day in Church history when Jesus stopped before a social outcast, and said, "Follow me." Matthew traded his tarnished treasures and personal ambition for accumulating inappropriate assets, for a place in the kingdom of heaven. Matthew learned that there is more to life than the multiplication of stocks and bonds, as proper as that might be at the right time and place. But there is more. There are eternal souls to be saved. There are people bound in sin to be set free. There is a Lord and Master to follow.

No one who has ever fully followed Christ has been sorry. Matthew never regretted leaving the custom's gate, because he received the fullness of the Holy Spirit who inspired him to write a gospel narrative that shall live and abide forever. The gospel of Matthew is the gift of grace from a grateful heart.

Like so many of the Apostles, the end of Matthew's life is full of legend and myth. Only two facts seem certain when all the evidence is considered: Matthew ministered to the saints in Egypt, and he met a violent death, killed by a sword wound, for preaching the gospel. Death by violence in Ethiopia came (c. A.D. 60) because from the moment that he arose to follow the Lord, Matthew never turned back to his old life. If there are spiritual lessons to be learned from the gospel narrative, they are familiar ones.

Christ calls some, not all, but some to sacrifice wealth, and occupation for an unknown and dangerous journey. The Church of Christ has many examples of individuals who re-evaluated their lives, and made adjustments to engage in the work of the Lord. Hudson Taylor, founder of the China Inland Mission, offers one example. In more recent years, Dr. D. Martyn Lloyd-Jones is another example. Dr. Lloyd-Jones gave up a promising medical career in order to preach the gospel. This is not to say that all Christians should be missionaries or ministers of the gospel. It is to say that God asks more from some than from others. Nevertheless, a desire to follow Christ should prevail in the heart of every person who names the name of Christ. Then, when time and opportunity arise, much good can be done for the cause of Christ.

Christ always meets with people where they are, not where they should be. Matthew was hurting others financially when Jesus halted his self-destructive and other destructive behavior. Saul of Tarsus was hurting others physically when Christ arrested his hatred of Christians. The woman of Samaria was hurting herself personally when Jesus spoke to her about her infidelity, and then her immortal soul. Christ went to people where they were, and called them to be different. The Church must be willing to do the same. The Church must love sinners, while hating sin. Christ will show mercy to all. Publicans and prostitutes, the proud and the passionate, can know something about a Savior who cares enough for them to come and say, "Follow me." And the heart remembers; it is a Person that is to be followed, not a program or even perceived prejudices.

Christ honors those who have dishonored themselves. He makes fallen men and women apostles, and fellow servants in His kingdom. In fact, He makes them kings and priests forever unto the living God.

Christ opened Himself up to misunderstanding. By eating and drinking with the Publicans and prostitutes, the Lord was not endorsing their lifestyle. Rather, He was calling them to repentance in His own way, the way of goodness and grace, not judgment and condemnation. The Bible teaches that the goodness of God leads men to repent. That is a wonderful spiritual lesson to remember.

Christ changes the heart so that Christians want to give, and keep on giving to others. Bro. Shelton, formerly of Mt. Zion Ministries in Florida, has spoken often of the joy of giving the gospel away free of charge. Freely he has received, and freely he gives, knowing that no one can out give God.

The example of Christ, and the example of the Apostles teach Christians to use every means to minister to others. There is a wonderful book that was written many years ago, *The Shoes of the Fisherman.* The highlight of the book comes when an obscure priest is elevated to the papacy. As the newly-elected Pope, he makes a public vow to spend his time dismantling the royal riches of the Vatican in order to be more like Christ and the apostles in their original state, rich in spirit. The Pope promises to help the poor and needy, to lift up the fallen, and to give comfort to those who are hurting.

A longing to help others is natural to the Christian heart, for it reflects the compassion of Christ Himself. Therefore, when the Lord brings different situations to our attention, let us do immediately what we can to help. Let us rise up as a Church and follow Christ to minister to others. We cannot help everyone, but we can help someone. We cannot proclaim the gospel everywhere, but we can spread the word somewhere. We cannot witness to all, but we can tell our friends and family about the Lord. We cannot give up everything we own or make, but we can give up something for the cause of the Kingdom, and the good of others.

In the act of giving we remember that we cannot serve both God and money. We cannot just take in and not give out. As we choose to serve God and to help others. We transform the treasures of time. Amen.

8

The Trials and Tribulations of St. Thomas

"Then said Jesus unto them plainly, Lazarus is dead. [15] And I am glad for your sakes that I was not there, to the intent ye may believe; nevertheless let us go unto him. [16] Then said Thomas, which is called Didymus, unto his fellow disciples, Let us also go, that we may die with him" (John 11:14–16; cf. 14:1–7; 20:19–31).

"Reputation is what men and women think of us; character is what God and angels know of us." —Thomas Paine

Throughout Church history, Thomas has been given the reputation of a man of great doubts. There is a measure of truth to the title, Doubting Thomas, but there is also an element of defamation implied. Perhaps Thomas can be rescued from the unfortunate epitaph.

Consider first the simple facts of Scripture. In the gospels of Matthew, Mark, and Luke, nothing is said about Thomas except his name. In the gospel of John, Thomas becomes a distinct and vivid character. John refers to him as, Thomas who is called Didymus. While Thomas is a Hebrew name, Didymus is a Greek name, meaning, twin. Understanding this, the early Christian community went into a frenzy of activity trying to discover whom Thomas might be a twin with. The most interesting interpretation is found in an early writing called The Acts of Thomas. The apocryphal story declares that Thomas was none other than the twin brother of Jesus Himself (3:1).

Turning to the Word of God, some more believable things are discovered about Thomas, such as his personal courage. This particular characteristic comes out in the wonderful story of Lazarus being raised from the dead in the town of Bethany (John 11:1–16).

Bethany [lit. House of Figs or, House of Affliction] was located close to Jerusalem. It was here that Lazarus grew sick, and suddenly died. Word came to the Lord about the death of Lazarus. And Jesus decided to go to the graveside of His friend. But the decision to journey to Bethany alarmed the disciples.

The disciples knew that the Lord's popularity with the religious leaders in Jerusalem was in trouble. A death threat had been issued against Christ. Already, on two occasions Jesus had been subject to stoning (John 8:59; 10:31). So to venture near Jerusalem appeared foolish, and even suicidal. As the thoughts of bloodshed and violence crossed the minds of the disciples, Thomas finally settled the matter by saying, Let us also go, that we may die with him.

Thomas was serious. He was determined not to be disloyal, and so he demonstrated the integrity of his heart by going on with Jesus. His courage inspired the other disciples to stay with the Savior as well. The courage of one man became the courage of many.

In English history, it is said that the presence of Oliver Cromwell on the field of battle was worth 10,000 soldiers. The courage of one man became the courage of many. In the chronicles of Texas, there is the narrative of something that took place during the siege of the Alamo. The Alamo was a mission fortress in San Antonio, Texas. Within its walls, during the Revolution of 1836, a band of Texans made a heroic resistance against an overwhelming Mexican army. The encounter began in December of 1835 when a small Texas force captured and occupied the fortress. The co-commanding officers of the garrison were Colonel William B. Travis, 26 years old, and James Bowie. David Crockett was also in the fort with some of his boys from the hills of Tennessee.

The scene was set for battle when, on February 23, 1836, General Antonio Lopez de Santa Anna began to place 6,000 Mexican soldiers around the fort. Defending the Alamo were 184 men. On March 5, Colonel Travis realized that the garrison was doomed. Replacements would never reach the mission in time. Assembling the men in the courtyard, Travis described their desperate plight. Then, he drew a line in the dirt with his sword and invited those who wished to cross and remain until the end to do so. The rest were free to try to escape from the Mexican army or surrender to it. All but one man crossed the line in a heroic decision to stay.

During the next thirteen days, the 183 defenders of the fort died. Those who stayed had crossed a line, literally, to stand and make the ultimate sacrifice for the cause of freedom. The courage of one man became the courage of many. The Church of Christ today needs men and women and young people of courage to inspire others because the enemies of the Church are real , and they are many in number. They are also deadly. Loyalty to the cause of Christ is essential, even unto death. Thomas was courageous, and he was loyal under adverse conditions. He made a great decision to die, even though that was not going to happen at the moment.

There is a wonderful and true story of a little boy whose sister needed a blood transfusion. The doctor explained that she had the same disease the boy had recovered from two years earlier. Her only chance of recovery was a transfusion from someone who had previously conquered the disease. Since the two children had the same rare blood type, the boy was an ideal donor. Would you give your blood to Mary? the doctor asked, and was surprised when Johnny hesitated. His lower lip started to tremble. Then he smiled and said, Sure, for my sister. Soon the two children were wheeled into the hospital room. Mary, pale and thin. Johnny, robust and healthy. Neither spoke, but when their eyes met, Johnny grinned. As the nurse inserted the needle into his arm, Johnny's smile faded. He watched as the blood flowed through the tube.

When the ordeal was almost over, Johnny's voice, slightly shaky, broke the silence. Doctor, when do I die? Only then did the doctor realize that why Johnny had initially hesitated, and why his lip had trembled when he agreed to donate his blood. He thought that by giving up his blood to his sister he was giving up his life for her. In that brief moment, he had made his great decision.

There was a brief moment when Thomas made his great decision. And he said, Let us also go, that we may die with him. As Thomas was a man brave of heart, he was also a man who could become honestly confused. He tried to understand what Christ was teaching, but at times it was not at all clear. Jesus spoke of crowns and kingdoms, yet, when people came by force to make Him a king, the Lord withdrew from their presence. Christ spoke of being God and He demonstrated the powers of divinity often. However, the Lord also spoke of suffering, crucifixion, death and dying (John 14:1–8). Should divine kings talk in such a manner? Thomas was not clear as to what it all meant.

Then there was the night of the Passover. In the Upper Room during the third Passover the Lord celebrated with His disciples, Jesus spoke of the Cross and what lay beyond that. He spoke of going away. But the spiritual truths were not understood by Thomas, or by anyone else. The minds of the disciples were spiritually dull. They could not understand the great mystery of which the Lord spoke. Thomas was listening. He wanted to comprehend everything, but the best Thomas could do was to interrupt and express his personal frustration. Lord, said Thomas, We know not where you are going; and how can we know the way.

The Lord was gracious. He did not rebuke Thomas in a harsh manner for his spiritual confusion. Jesus merely explained the basics of the Christian faith one more time. Thomas, remember I have taught you, I am the way, I am the truth, and the life. Thomas, No man cometh unto the Father but by me. Do you understand? Thomas did not understand. Later he would perceive just what Jesus meant in all of His messages. For the moment, it was enough to be in the presence of the Lord. And so it is, to believe in Christ, to know Him, to love Him, to trust Him, that is all that really matters. To know Christ is to know the way to heaven, and to have fellowship with the Father.

There is a negative side to Thomas that cannot be avoided. He was a man who found it difficult to believe when the dark clouds of life gathered about him. When Jesus died on the Cross, Thomas was devastated. Though he had been taught that Christ was to come out of the grave on the third day, he simply did not believe it would happen. All of the miracles he had witnessed, all of the sermons from the lips of the Lord, all of the private conversations did not sustain him in the hour of spiritual testing. Even when he heard that the resurrected Lord appeared to the other disciples, he did not believe, and that is a terrible thing. Obstinate unbelief in the face of irrefutable evidence is a terrible thing. Said Thomas, Except I shall see in his hands the print of the nails, And put my finger into the print of the nails, And thrust my hand into his side, I will not believe.

Here is unbelief that is bold. Except Thomas was allowed to physically touch the resurrected Christ he was not going to believe. In condescending grace, the Lord came to Thomas and was willing to let His disciple touch Him (John 20:26–27). That will not happen again, for the Lord went on to say, Blessed are they that have not seen and yet have believed. By the mercy of God, you and I do not have to physically touch a nail-scarred hand in order to believe. But, like Thomas, we must have a very real and personal encounter with the Living Lord Jesus. Christ is not a theory, but the Living Lord.

Dr. William Barclay in *The Master's Men*, offers two great lessons from the Scriptural narrative of the life of Thomas in the New Testament. The first lesson is that Jesus blames no man, or woman, or young person for wanting to be certain concerning the claims of Christ. There is nothing sinful about wanting to be convinced that Christianity is genuine. C. S. Lewis was a thorough skeptic before he met the Master. But he was an honest skeptic, and one day the Lord broke through his doubts to fill him with faith. It is not wrong to have doubts, but it is extremely wrong to continue to doubt when truth is revealed.

A second great lesson from the life of Thomas, is that certainty is most likely to come to a person in the fellowship of other believers. The world is waiting, almost with bated breath, for the confessing Church to embrace its profession of faith. Many a person has turned away from the Church because the reality of a Christian's life does not match the religious rhetoric. The divine solution is for the Church to have a spiritual renewal by encountering once more, by faith, the Living Lord. Historically, that is called revival. When revival comes, individuals will want to meet often with one another to tell what God is doing in their lives all the days they live. Malachi 3:16 says, "Then they that feared the Lord spake often one to another: and the Lord hearkened, and heard it, and a book of remembrance was written before him for them that feared the Lord, and they thought upon his name."

Tradition records that Thomas ministered in South India, and there met a violent death. The principal document for this tradition is The Acts of Thomas, which has been preserved from c. A.D. 220 with some variations both in Greek and in Syriac. The narrative of the document is totally exaggerated, but there is at least one seed of truth that might be reflected in the manuscript. According to tradition, the apostles agreed to go in different directions to evangelize the world. By a casting of lots, large geographical territories were assigned to the Apostles. India fell to Thomas, but he declared his inability to go. As a result, Christ appeared in a supernatural way to Abban, the ambassador of Gundafor, an Indian king, and sold Thomas to him to be his slave. Thomas was to serve Gundafor as a carpenter. Then Abban and Thomas sailed away until they came to Andrapolis, where they landed and attended the marriage feast of the ruler's daughter. Strange occurrences followed, and Christ, assuming the appearance of Thomas, exhorted the bride to remain a Virgin.

Coming to India, Thomas was given money to build a palace for Gundafor, but instead he used the money to minister to the poor. In anger, Gundafor imprisoned him; but the Apostle escaped miraculously, and Gundafor was converted.

Traveling throughout the country preaching the gospel, Thomas met with strange adventures as he allegedly encountered dragons, and wild asses. Then he came to the city of King Misdai (Syriac, Mazdai) where he was able to win to Christ the wife of Misdai, Tertia, and their son, Vazan. Because of this, Thomas was condemned to death. He was led out of the city to a hill, and pierced through with spears by four soldiers. He was then buried in the tomb of the ancient kings, but his remains were afterwards removed to the West. The tradition that St. Thomas preached in India has been widely accepted by the church in both East and West. Perhaps the greatest thing that can be said about Thomas is that he served the Savior, and is worthy of receiving the crown of life.

The total life of Thomas, with all of its trials and tribulations, serves to remind the Church that the Christian way of life is very challenging. Jesus never said it would be any different. In fact, the Lord told those who wanted to follow Him to count the cost. He told everyone that He was going to die on a cross, and that those who came after Him must pick up their cross as well. The Lord warned that not all would remain faithful (Matt. 13:3b–9; cf. 13:18–23). However, those who endure to the end in the sphere of faith shall know the joy of entering into the presence of God. Are you enduring to the end? Will you be found faithful? These are not idle questions, for there are many ways to lose our faith. The world, the flesh, and the devil, have united to destroy and damn as many souls as possible. Therefore, everything must be done to preserve and protect the delicate flower of faith from perishing.

Faith is preserved and protected when known sin is immediately confessed before God, not only on a daily basis, but as often as necessary. Psalm 32:5 says, "I acknowledged my sin unto thee, and mine iniquity have I not hid. I said, I will confess my transgressions unto the Lord; and thou forgavest the iniquity of my sin."

Faith is preserved and protected when the Scriptures are meditated upon morning, noon, and night. Psalm 119:10, "With my whole heart have I sought thee: O let me not wander from thy commandments."

Faith is preserved and protected when the means of grace are availed, such as regular attendance at worship, and taking of communion. Psalm 5:7, "But as for me, I will come into thy house in the multitude of thy mercy; and in thy fear will I worship toward thy holy temple."

Faith is preserved and protected when personal standards are established and honored. Romans 12:1–2, "I beseech you therefore brethren, by the mercies of God, that ye present your bodies a living sacrifice, holy, acceptable, unto God, And be not conformed to this world: but be ye transformed by the renewing of your mind, that ye may prove what is that good, and acceptable and perfect will of God."

Faith is preserved and protected when the gospel is shared with others, for this is the will of the Lord. Acts 1:8, "But ye shall receive power, after that the Holy Ghost is come upon you: and ye shall be witnesses unto me both in Jerusalem, and in all Judea and in Samaria, and unto the uttermost part of the earth."

Faith is preserved and protected when the heart is guarded against secret or subtle sins, such as bitterness, hatred, jealousy, anger, lust, pride, and greed. Hebrews 12:15, "Looking diligently lest any man fail of the grace of God; lest any root of bitterness springing up trouble you, and thereby many be defiled."

Faith is protected when the face of the Lord is sought in earnest. May God grant His church grace, corporately and individually, to preserve and protect the faith that we profess to possess in Christ Jesus our Lord. A life of faith preserved and protected because it is rooted in a heart of faith pleases God.

9

James: The Second Son of Alphaeus

"Now the names of the twelve apostles are these; . . . and Matthew the publican . . ." (Matt. 10:2–3; cf. Mark 3:18; Luke 6:15; Acts 1:13).

Once again we are faced with the challenge of studying an apostle about which little is known except His name. Once again we are forced to remember a practical principle, the message is more important than the man, even an apostle. A.W. Tozer once preached a sermon entitled "What Man is not to Glory in, and Why." His text was Jeremiah 9:23–24, which reads, "Thus saith the LORD, Let not the wise man glory in his wisdom, Neither let the mighty man glory in his might, let not the rich man glory in his riches . . . But let him that glorieth glory in this, That he understandeth and knoweth me, that I am the LORD Which exercise loving kindness, judgment, and righteousness, In the earth: for in these things I delight, saith the LORD."

There is good reason, explained Dr. Tozer, why the mighty man is not to glory in his might, or the wise man in his wisdom, or the rich man in his riches. The reason is simple. The wisest of all men are really not so wise. Who has yet to explain the origin of life and the universe? While there are great advances in information, each door of knowledge that opens reveals a more complex and immense field of study.

In like manner, the mighty man is not so mighty. At the beginning of the last century, in 1927, when Jack Dempsey was fighting Gene Tunney for the heavyweight championship of the world, the event was billed as the "fight of the century." One honest sports commentator was not impressed and made the observation that a half-grown gorilla could whip both contenders with no problem at all.

Living in a day that glorified the athlete and the power of the gladiators, Paul reminded people that bodily exercise profiteth little. There is some profit, but exercising to holiness is more important. And the rich person should not boast in wealth. The One who gave it can take it away suddenly, or He can take the person from the money. In 1988, the death of Christina Onaiases was reported. She died at the age of 37. Though the heiress of billions of dollars, she was not able to function normally in life. Drugs did not help. Four marriages did not help. Like others before her, Christina was a "poor little rich girl," and she exited from life in a tragic way.

Power, education, physical beauty, money, or being an apostle must not be glorified in. Rather, a person can only glory in understanding and knowing the Lord Jesus Christ as personal Savior. Jesus told the apostles not to rejoice in their abilities to heal the sick or raise the dead, but Rejoice because your names are written in heaven (Luke 10:20). If we know little about the apostle James, it is enough that his name is written in the Lamb's Book of Life.

However, there are some things that can be said about James. Through careful study of the Scriptures, three probable conclusions can be reached. First, he is the brother of Matthew. James is consistently identified as the Son of Alphaeus. Mark tells us that Matthew (Levi) was also the son of Alphaeus. Many Bible scholars are in agreement that Matthew and James were brothers, but they were brothers who violently disagreed over politics and religion.

Matthew chose to unite with the Roman Empire in order to take money from his own people through taxation. As a result, he brought shame to his religious heritage and family tribe, which was the priestly tribe of Levi. In contrast, it may be that James chose to identify himself with the Zealots. The Zealots were a fanatical patriotic Jewish group whose single purpose was to overthrow the rule of Rome through every means, including terrorist activity. The evidence that James was at one time a member of this terrorist organization is slight, but interesting. In the list of the apostles given by Matthew, Mark, and Luke, four disciples are consistently named together.

- James the son of Alphaeus
- Thaddaeus (Judas, the brother of James)
- Simon the Zealot
- Judas Iscariot

In ancient documents each of these men are linked to the Zealots in some form. If James was the brother of Matthew as the son of Alphaeus, and if he was a member of the Zealots, then there must have been some intense hostility in the home of Alphaeus. One son was considered to be a traitor to Israel, while the other son was constantly subject to Roman arrest. And yet they came together to follow Christ. It is a wonderful testimony to the fact that Jesus came not only to reconcile men to God, but also, at times, to reconcile people to each other. There is not always a happy ending to conflict within families. The place of pledged love often becomes a battle ground for the launching of verbal, mental, and physical abuse. The Bible is realistic. There is sometimes much danger within families. There is much hatred and hostility as individuals try to control the behavior of others. The Holy Spirit faithfully records the unspeakable.

- Cain killed his brother Abel.
- Jacob robbed his brother Esau, and lied to their father Isaac.
- Even the Lord's own brothers and sisters thought that He was mad for claiming to be the Messiah.

Jesus said that He came to put a sword in the home and divide husband and wife, father, and son, mother and daughter. Some of the greatest opposition to the cause of Christ comes from family members. However, there is also the reality that when individuals submit to the Lord Jesus as Master, He has a wonderful way of transforming hearts. No longer do people need, or want to hurt each other. They can be gracious again. It has been noted that a hundred pianos tuned to one instrument are tuned to one another, and a hundred Christians following Christ will care for one another.

Here is a great lesson: If Christian grace is to reign in a relationship, then individuals must first of all be in love with Christ. The Lord can restore a broken relationship when He is honored and the principles of 1 Corinthians 13 are seriously applied to specific situations. The working together of a political zealot and a pawn of greed, demonstrate the power of Christ, and the gospel of redeeming grace.

Whatever else is known about James, the son of Alphaeus, is shrouded in legend and tradition. One interesting story has been preserved in the Golden Legend, a seven volume collection of events in the lives of the saints dating back to A.D. 1275. The legend relates that James resembled Jesus Christ so much in his physical appearance that it was difficult to tell them apart, which is why Judas kissed the Lord in the Garden of Gethsemane. The killing kiss of Judas was to make sure that Jesus, and not James, was taken prisoner. Having spent three and half intense years with Christ, maybe James did begin to look like Jesus. Certainly it was his desire to be like Christ. That is a worthy objective of every believer.

> O to be like Thee! Blessed Redeemer,
>> This is my constant longing and prayer,
> Gladly I'll forfeit all of earth's treasures,
>> Jesus, Thy perfect likeness to wear.

Tradition records that James preached in Persia, and that he died a martyr by crucifixion. The word martyr literally means, witness. James was a witness for the Lord until the end of time. There are two basic ways to witness for Christ: by life, and by lips. The life of a Christian ought to be different in public, and in private, from the life of a person unconverted. There are certain things Christians should not do because they are fundamentally wrong. And there are certain things Christians should do because they are right. The fruit of the Spirit can be manifested, such as love, joy, peace, gentleness, goodness, meekness, and self-control.

In addition to being a witness by living a virtuous life, there is the matter of the lips. The Bible says that faith cometh by hearing and hearing by the Word of God. But how shall people hear unless Christians witness to them and tell them the gospel? In Acts 8, the story is told how all the Church was persecuted by Saul and had to hide for protection. Therefore, they that were scattered abroad went everywhere preaching the word. It is the church as a whole that must preach the Word of God, and not just a select few. This point is essential to understand, because it puts a responsibility on every man, woman, and young person, to somehow, somewhere, tell others that Jesus Christ is Lord.

Being an effective witness for Christ takes desire and sensitivity, but the Lord will have His people witness for Him. He has given us apostles as examples. They, in turn, have given us their own lives to encourage our hearts to go forth with the good news of saving grace. We must do something for Christ whether we are remembered in detail or not. The truth of the matter is that most of us, says Dr. Herbert Lockyer, are commonplace, having no exceptional gifts or powers. We are inconspicuous, simple, ordinary folk, models of mediocrity. Yet the commonplace character of our limitations should not make us indifferent about living to the full in our small corner. Much of the world's most needed, and most blessed work is done by those about whom the world knows nothing.

The Baptism of the Believer

Without question, the best starting place to be a witness for Christ by life and by lip is in the act of baptism. Baptism is the will of the Lord. It is His holy command, and so is not to be neglected or ignored. While it is true that baptism does not save in and of itself, and while it is true that baptism does not keep a person saved, it is also true that baptism is commanded. In Matthew 28:18–20, Jesus said, "All power is given unto me in heaven and in earth. Go ye therefore, and teach all nations, baptizing them in the name of the Father, and of the Son, and of the Holy Ghost: Teaching them to observe all things whatsoever I have commanded you: and lo, I am with you alway, even unto the end of the world. The Church has no option but to obey the will of the Lord."

Every Christian has a Great Commission: To teach all nations, and to be taught the things of the Lord; to baptize all disciples, and to be baptized as well; to disciple others in the doctrines of grace, and to be students of the Word as well.

In the act of baptism several things happen. First, the Lordship of Christ is honored. Many years ago, a number of prominent literary men were assembled in a plush clubroom in London. The conversation was directed to a discussion of some of the important figures of the past, and one of the company suddenly asked: Gentlemen, what would we do if Milton were to enter this room? Ah, replied one of the men, we would give him such an ovation as might compensate for the delayed recognition accorded him by the men of his own generation. And if Shakespeare entered? Asked another. We would arise and crown him master of song, was the answer. And if Jesus Christ were to enter? Asked another. I think, said Charles Lamb amid an intense silence, we would all fall on our faces. If Jesus has all regal power, and if Jesus has all saving power, then obviously He is to be obeyed. It is the will of Christ for His subjects to be baptized. It is the will of the Savior for those for whom He has died to be baptized because in the act of submission to baptism His Lordship is recognized.

Second, in the act of baptism a spiritual symbolism is expressed. By going down into the water, the believer is buried in the likeness of His death. And when the person comes up out of the water, he is raised in the likeness of His resurrection. By the act of baptism every believer is identified with the substitutionary death of Christ. We do not have to die at Calvary, but Christ did. We do not have to go to hell to atone for sins, but Christ did. He took our pain and our just penalty in His own body, and He asks us to identify with Him in that great work of redemption.

Third, in the act of baptism, the world knows that there is no turning back. This was certainly true for the early Jewish converts who came to Christ. By baptism, they made a dramatic break with the past. Many Christians who have come out of cultic structures, or the occult, experience the same radical cleavage. And there is no going back.

Fourth, in the act of baptism, the experience is such that it shall never be forgotten. There is a feeling of being born again because all sins have been washed away.

A ruler once came to Jesus by night,
  To ask Him the way of salvation and light;
The Master made answer in words true and plain,

Ye must be born again
Ye must be born again
Ye must be born again
  I verily, verily say unto thee,
Ye must be born again.

Nothing illustrates the new birth better than the act of baptism.

Finally, in the act of baptism, great humility is revealed. It is somewhat embarrassing to be baptized, because it does not happen every day. New situations are always a little uncomfortable for most people. But Jesus said, "If you do not confess Me before men, neither will I confess you before my Father who is in heaven." To be ashamed of Christ is unthinkable for a Christian.

If you have never been obedient to the will of the Lord in baptism, then do not delay. By life and by lip, by private conversations and public demonstrations, tell the world you are a Christian so you can sing with sincerity,

I'll tell the world that I'm a Christian—
  I'm not ashamed His name to bear;

I'll tell the world that I'm a Christian—
   I'll take Him with me anywhere.

I'll tell the world how Jesus saved me,
   And how He gave me a life brand new;
And I know that if you trust Him
   That all He gave me
He'll give you.

I'll tell the world that He's my Savior,
   No other one could love me so;
My life, my all is His forever,
   And where He leads me
I will go.

10

The Last Question from the Lips of Thaddaeus

Judas saith unto him, not Iscariot, Lord, how is it that thou wilt manifest thyself unto us, and not unto the world?" (John 14:22).

St. Jerome called the tenth apostle Trinomius, which means the man with three names. In the Gospel of Mark, he is called Thaddaeus (Mark 3:18); in Matthew he is called Lebbaeus, whose surname was Thaddaeus (Matt. 10:3); and in Luke he is called Judas, the brother of James (Luke 6:16; cf. Acts 1:13). Like several of the other apostles little is known of Thaddaeus, but what is known is significant. In the first three gospels only a name is given. It is in the fourth gospel that one brief cameo appearance is made of the man under the name of Judas, not Iscariot (John 14:22). The holy Author is careful not to confuse the two men, for one would become a saint, while the other would remain a son of the Accuser.

The scene that is set forth in John 14 takes place at the Last Supper. Jesus had been speaking about going away. It was obvious to all that He was disturbed and this caused concern to the disciples. Why was Jesus going away? Where was He going?

What was He trying to say? The disciples did not understand. What the disciples understood was that the Lord was the promised Messiah. But they also thought that He had come to overthrow the Roman government and set up His own earthly political kingdom. Just when the Lord was going to do this was uncertain. In fact, the disciples had often discussed this important point. They wondered when Christ would reveal to the masses His power and program.

Sensing an opportune moment had come to clarify the issues at stake, Thaddaeus raised a question of concern indirectly. Lord, he asked, how is it that thou wilt manifest thyself unto us, and not unto the world? The question is an interesting one and offers insight into the hearts of the disciples. The question reflects a failure on the part of the apostles to understand the basic teachings of Jesus. The disciples had failed to comprehend the ultimate implications of the ministry of the Messiah. Had Judas Thaddaeus and the others been given a report card for spiritual perception, they would have failed. For three years Jesus had been communicating certain concepts to His disciples.

All of humanity needs a Savior. Every person born into the world is a son or daughter of Adam with the judgment of sin stamped on the soul. Jesus said that out of the heart proceed evil thoughts, murders, adulteries, fornications, thefts, false witness, blasphemies; These are the things which defile a man (Matt. 15:19–20a). But He also said that the Son of Man is come to seek and to save that which was lost (Luke 19:10). The Pharisees did not want to hear this, and reacted in a violent manner. They sought to kill Christ and, in the end, thought they had succeeded.

Salvation is based upon sovereign electing grace, not human merit or self-effort. On the night of His birth the angels announced to the shepherds the divine work of redemption. Christ had come, they said, to save His people from their sins (Matt. 1:21). His people are those whom the Father has given to Him (John 17:6). In other passages this truth is set forth in the doctrine of predestination (Eph. 1:4–5; 1:11; Rom. 8:29).

The Son of God would secure the redemption of lost souls by offering Himself as a personal substitute for sinners. Behold, we go up to Jerusalem; and the Son of Man shall be betrayed unto the chief priests and unto the scribes, and they shall condemn Him to death, And shall deliver Him to the Gentiles to mock, and to scourge, and to crucify Him: and the third day He shall rise again (Matt. 20:18–19). The Cross was central to the life of Christ, and it is central to the life of all who would be cleansed from the pollution of sin. William Cowper understood this spiritual truth and wrote of the purity that comes to those who go to the Cross.

> There is a fountain filled with blood
> > Drawn from Emmanuel's veins'
> And sinners plunged beneath that flood,
> > Lose all their guilty stains.

With His redeemed, Christ would establish a spiritual kingdom. My kingdom is not of this world, He said (John

18:36). The kingdom Christ came to build is in the hearts of those to whom He would reveal Himself.

But why would the Lord reveal Himself to the few, and not to the many? Lebbaeus Judas Thaddaeus wanted to know, and so he asked very plainly, Lord, how is it that Thou wilt manifest thyself unto us and not unto the world? And the divine response came. Thaddaeus, many are called to salvation, but only few are chosen (Matt. 22:14). Thaddaeus, my sheep will hear my voice and I know them, and they follow Me (John 10:27). And a truth is realized. Only those to whom God has revealed Himself through His Son are counted among the elect. The elect of God are those that will enjoy eternal life while serving the Savior in the sphere of the kingdom of heaven. This favor is not for everyone in the world, but only for those whom the Father has given to the Son.

Have you ever considered what life would be like without Christ? Some people know all too well. *First*, a life without God is a life without meaning. The old catechisms teach that the chief end of man is to know God and to enjoy Him forever. There is truth in that teaching. We are created for a purpose. *Second*, a life without God is a life without hope. There is no hope of any life beyond the grave, and thus no hope of heaven. *Third*, a life without God is a life of foolish distractions. The days may be filled with work and the pursuit of wealth, there may be family and friends to enjoy, and travel, but at the end of one's days it will all seem foolish in light of eternity. The parable of Christ in Luke 12:13–21 illustrates this point. A life without God is a life of wasted years. What a difference there is for those who are to be the heirs of salvation. They have a meaning to life, hope for the future, and the joy of serving the Savior as the heirs of salvation.

The heirs of salvation can be easily identified. Jesus said, "If a man love me, He will keep my words." With these words the Lord provided the best motive for living out the ethics of the Christian life: love for Christ. This point is vital to remember, for motives are important. They always have been (cf. Gen. 4), and they always will be. God is interested in what individuals do, and in why they do what they do. The motive for being a Christian should be pure and unselfish in nature. However, this is not always the case. Sometimes people come to Christ for the wrong reason.

Some people come to Christ because they want power over others. That was true in the case of Simon, as recorded in the book of Acts (8:9–21): "But there was a certain man, called Simon, which before time in the same city used sorcery, and bewitched the people of Samaria, giving out that he himself was some great one. To whom they all gave heed, from the least to the greatest, saying, This man is the great power of God. And to him they had regard, because that of long time he had bewitched them with sorceries. . . . And when Simon saw that through laying on of the apostle's hands the Holy Ghost was given, he offered them money, Saying, give me also this power, that on whomsoever I lay hands, he may receive the Holy Ghost. But Peter said unto him, Thy money perish with thee, because thou hast thought that the gift of God may be purchased with money. Thou has neither part nor lot in this matter: for thy heart is not right in the sight of God."

Some people come to Christ, not out of love for His substitutionary death, but out of a fear of a future judgment. There are those who have been wounded in their conscience over certain sins. They have heard the threats, and curses, and warnings of condemnation, and so they come seeking divine forgiveness. But soon after making a confession of faith, Christianity becomes a religion without joy, and the Church is forsaken. Why? Because there was no love for Christ. There was only a personal desire to escape the pain of a wounded conscience.

In contrast to those who would come to Christ for ulterior motives, there are others who are inspired to serve and sacrifice for the Savior because they love Him. Those who are truly born again have a natural love for Christ, which reveals itself in words and deeds of spiritual service. 'If you love me, said Jesus, you will keep my words.

There is something else. Jesus promised that those who love Him and keep His words shall know in a special way the presence of Himself and the Father. If a man love me, he will keep my words: and my Father will love him, and we will come unto him, and make our abode with him (John 14:23b). This is possible through the indwelling of the Holy Spirit.

In a real, but mysterious way, God the Holy Spirit comes to indwell every redeemed soul. Then, little by little He teaches about the Son and the Father. Spiritual truths are grasped. They are simple at first.

The Bible is the inspired Word of God. All Scripture is given by inspiration of God, and is profitable for doctrine, for reproof, for correction, for instruction in righteousness: That the man of God may be perfect, thoroughly furnished unto all good works (2 Tim. 3:16).

Salvation is by grace through faith alone. "For by grace are ye saved through faith; and that not of yourselves: it is the gift of God: Not of works, lest any many should boast" (Eph. 2:8–9).

A holy life is a life of standards. "For ye were sometimes darkness, but now are ye light in the Lord: walk as children of light" (Eph. 5:18).

Death is certain. "For it is appointed unto men once to die" (Heb. 9:27). Preparation must be made to meet God (Amos 4:12).

There is a Day of Judgment. "For we must all appear before the judgment seat of Christ" (Rom. 14:10; 2 Cor. 5:10).

As time goes on, the Christian begins to learn about the deeper things of God. The glorious doctrines of predestination, election, and justification are comprehended. There is growth in grace and in knowledge of the Lord Jesus Christ. And all this comes because from the sea of humanity the Lord has been pleased to reveal Himself to the few, if not to the many. Lord, how is it that Thou wilt manifest thyself unto us and not unto the world? And the answer is sovereign grace.

History closes the book on this apostle, except for a lovely legend that tells of a correspondence between Jesus and a man named Abgarus, who was King of Edessa, a city in Northern

Mesopotamia near the Euphrates. The letter begins with these words: Abgarus, ruler of Edessa, to Jesus the excellent Savior who has appeared in the country of Jerusalem, greeting. I have heard the reports of thee and of thy cures as performed by thee without medicine and without herbs. For it is said that thou makest the blind to see and the lame to walk, that thou cleansest lepers and casteth out impure spirits and demons, and that thou healest those afflicted with lingering diseases, and raisest the dead. And having heard all these things concerning thee, I have concluded that one of two things must be true: either thou art God, and having come down from heaven thou doest these things or else, thou who doest these things art the Son of God. I have therefore written to thee to ask thee that thou wouldst take the trouble to come to me and heal the disease, which I have. For I have heard that the Jews are murmuring against thee and are plotting to injure thee. But I have a very small yet noble city, which is big enough for us both. The reply is given.

The Answer of Jesus to the ruler Abgarus by the courier Ananias. Blessed art thou who hast believed in me without having seen me. For it is written concerning me that they who have seen me will not believe in me, and that they who have not seen me will believe and be saved. But in regard to what thou hast written to me, that I should come to thee, it is necessary for me to fulfill all things here for which I have been sent, and after I have fulfilled them thus to be taken up again to him that sent me. But after I have been taken up I will send thee one of my disciples, that he may heal thy disease, and give life to thee and to thine.

There is more to the legend, but the story is understood. It was the work of Thaddaeus, as it was the work of all the apostles, to spread the good news of Jesus Christ. Surely Thaddaeus did that. Because of his service for the Savior souls came to faith. He was crucified in Persia (c. A.D. 72).

Judas Thaddaeus stands in stark contrast to Judas Iscariot. While one was false and treacherous, the other was steadfast and faithful. It is a wonderful attribute to be found faithful. The Bible exhorts Christians in this area.

Therefore, my beloved brethren, be ye steadfast, unmoveable, always abounding in the work of the Lord, forasmuch as ye know that your labor is not in vain in the Lord (1 Cor. 15:58). Jesus warned of those who would fall away from the faith (Matt. 13:1–9; cf. 13:18–23). The secret of success is constancy of purpose, said Disraeli, former Prime Minister of England. If you do not desire to resist the Devil, you will not resist him. If you do not seek to endure to the end, you will meet failure. If you do not desire to love God, you will stop short. It is easy to quit. It is tough to keep going.

In 1815, the Duke of Wellington (1769–1852) was talking to his forces at Waterloo. The great battle was on between himself and the French forces of Napoleon Bonaparte (1769–1821). Hard pounding this, Gentleman, he said. Let's see who can pound the longest! That is the secret of success. There is a wonderful story about Leonard de Vinci as he painted the picture of the Last Supper. A crowd watched over his shoulder. He was working on the fruit on the table, and he saw the crowd looking at his every movement. With one angry brush stroke he deliberately ruined the fruit. Pointing to the face of Christ he said, Don't look down there, look up here! When a man loves Jesus, he will follow the teachings of the Master. There is a need for Christians to commit themselves afresh to being steadfast in the will and the work of the Lord, just like Thaddaeus.

11

Simon the Zealot: Zealous for the Savior

"... and Simon called Zelotes," (Luke 6:15; cf. Matt. 10:4; Mark 3:18; Acts 1:13).

In order to fully appreciate the character of the apostle called Simon from Cana of Galilee, it will be necessary to understand the political climate of the day in which he lived. Palestine was a land under the rule of Rome. For centuries the Jews had been dominated by foreign powers. First there was the Babylonians. Then came the Medes and the Persians. After that the Greeks and the Romans took their place as a world empire. But in all the years of being under the heel of foreign domination, the Jews never got used to the mastery of others, and from time to time they managed to put together a revolt against their foreign oppression.

For example, in the second century BC there arose a family called the Maccabees, whose sole purpose was to make Israel a free and independent state. When Mattathias, the father of the Maccabees lay dying, his parting message was, "And now, my children, be zealous for the Law, and give your lives for the covenant of your fathers" (1 Macc. 2:50).

Time passed. Israel found herself still under foreign domination, and yet the flames of patriotism never died out. During the time of Christ, a group of people in Palestine banded together, remembered the word of Mattathias, and took for themselves the name of Zealots. Josephus describes them as a group. "They have an inviolable attachment to liberty, and say that God is only their Ruler and Lord. They do not mind dying any kind of death, nor do they heed the torture of their kindred and their friends, nor can any such fear make them call man lord."

Such fanatical zeal can easily be misguided and misapplied. There was a natural temptation to use patriotism as an opportunity for guerrilla warfare to burn and rob villages and towns. Wanton acts of destruction were excused and justified. The zealots were guilty of guerrilla warfare. They were also guilty of turning their weapons and violence against their own countrymen. Any Jew who appeared willing to compromise, or work with the Roman government was marked for destruction.

Some historians have suggested that the zealots were directly responsible for the most terrible time in ancient Jewish history. The story begins when Rome, tired of the social unrest in Palestine, decided to confront the Jews once and for all when another revolt broke out in Jerusalem in the summer of A.D. 66. To everyone's surprise, at first things did not go well for the Romans. A legion of soldiers was actually defeated by the Jews. The uprising became a full war.

Following the death of Nero, the new emperor, Vespasian, placed his son, Titus, in charge of challenging the Jewish uprising. Deciding that a strong, overwhelming military presence around

Jerusalem would be necessary, Titus circled the city with 80,000 men. Meanwhile, inside the walls of the ancient city civil war was taking place. Zealots and moderates were slaughtering each other as they fought for political control. Jewish blood flowed freely in the streets. Once more Titus demanded the surrender of the citadel, but the Jews laughed in defiance.

Growing impatient with the seizure of the city, and being prolonged month after month, Titus used the might of his military machines to literally pound a breach in the northern wall. Soon thereafter another wall was pierced and the Roman legions moved into part of the city. Fierce hand to hand fighting broke out. The body count began to mount rapidly.

Turning to psychological warfare, Titus tried to frighten those who remained in the city into submitting to his force. All the soldiers put on their best uniforms, polished their shields, and displayed their armor. But the Jews were still not impressed, nor were they intimidated. Nevertheless the end was in sight, for the food supply was running low. Titus had made sure this would happen by instituting a policy of forced starvation. Those who were caught outside the city walls trying to escape, or smuggle in supplies were crucified. For a while, about 500 people per day were being put on crosses. To find wood, every tree in the area for miles was cut down. Famine came to the city with a vengeance. Death was everywhere. Desperate with hunger, cannibalism broke out. Women boiled their children and ate them.

As the people grew physically weaker, the battering rams of the Romans continued to break down the walls. By the beginning of July, another part of the city fell. The Tower of Antonio, named in honor of Mark Anthony was in Roman hands. Nearby was the great Holy Temple. A soldier tossed a flaming torch through the Golden Windows into the Holy of Holies. Soon the sacred place of worship was in flames.

Titus had not wanted the Temple to be burnt, but the soldiers went out of control. The madness of war took its toll. In that terrible month of August, A.D. 70, Jerusalem was devastated as 97,000 prisoners were taken hostage and 115,800 corpses were removed from the city. And yet, despite all of this, some of the Zealots did not give up.

Prior to the final siege of Jerusalem, a large group managed to flee to a high fortress, called Masada. They were led by Eleazer. For two years this band of less than a 1,000 men, women, and children withstood 10,000 soldiers of the Roman army sent to subdue them. But their end was inevitable. The Roman General, Flavia Silva built a tremendous ramp on the other side of the mountain.

When it was finally clear that all hope of escape was gone, Eleazer summoned the people together in order to suggest a suicide pact. The people agreed to die, rather than submit to Roman slavery. The men tenderly embraced their wives, kissed their children, and then began the bloody work. Nine hundred and fifty perished, only two women and five children escaped by hiding in a cave. Ten men were appointed to slit the throats of the rest, and then they would be killed by one of their own. The last person alive was to commit suicide. Such were the Zealots. They were loyal, courageous, nationalistic, and in the end, unconquerable. Simon was a Zealot, until he came to Christ.

It is sometimes difficult to discover when or why a person begins to change in a radical way, for bad or for good. Since the New Testament tells us nothing about Simon except his name, it is not unreasonable to surmise that Simon came to Christ initially for political purposes. Perhaps Simon saw in Christ another Maccabee, or someone like Judas the Galilean, who led an insurrection following the death of Herod the Great in 4 B.C. After all, Jesus spoke of the Kingdom of God as being at hand. Perhaps Simon saw in Christ a political leader with supernatural power, to the point that He could raise the dead. Whatever attracted Simon to Jesus, the compelling character of the Lord, and the regenerating work of the Holy Spirit transformed Simon. The total transformation of Simon is manifested in several ways.

First, there is Simon's tolerance of Matthew. As a tax collector, Matthew was the type of person the Zealots looked for to assassinate with their little curved swords. The Zealots hated any Jew, with pure passion, who united with Rome to exploit their countrymen. In another time and place, Simon would have gladly slain Matthew. But they met as friends in the fellowship of the Savior. The very fact that Jesus was able to bring Matthew and Simon into one group demonstrates how personal enmity can be destroyed by a common love for Christ. Here is a great lesson for Christians in general, and the Church in particular. Christian love says, I will accept you as you are, and if you change, it will be because of your love for Christ (Dr. William Barclay).

Second, Simon's total transformation is reflected by the fact that he subordinated his earthly kingdom longings for the spiritual kingdom of heaven. In the pursuit of money, property, power, social status, and security, the soul must not be neglected. When all is said and done this truth remains: This one life shall soon be passed; only what is done for Christ will last. Jesus asked rhetorically, What shall it profit a man if he gain the whole world and lose his soul?

There is a third sign of a transformed life. Simon was found in the prayer meeting of Acts 1:13. In an Upper Room, Simon was found to be waiting for the power on high. In an Upper Room, Simon was found in prayer. The prayer life becomes the basis on which to judge the spiritual health of a soul. Not all of God's people are eloquent. Not all of God's people have prominent spiritual gifts. But all of God's people can pray. The more complete the transformation of the life, the more prayer will be displayed.

History does not record what happened to Simon. Even legend is vague about him. He is said to have preached in Egypt, in Africa, and even in Britain, until he met his death in Persia. Because of the opposition of two magicians, called Zaroes and Arfaxat, death came to Simon. He was crucified in the year A.D. 74. Dr. William Barclay notes, "Two things strike the investigator of early Christian history: the marvelous manner in which Christian seed is found growing and fructifying in unheard of places; the indifference of the sowers of perpetrating their own name and labors."

One day, in the providence of the Lord, the Church will visit again with this obscure apostle who had such a radical change of nature, and who was able to give his life for the greatest cause on earth , advancing the Kingdom of God. One reason why Simon was willing to dedicate his life to the service of the Savior, and the Church was because he saw the Church as the most glorious of all institutions. It is possible that many problems in local assemblies would be solved immediately if the Church was seen once more as a glorious institution. It is because of the lack of a fundamental respect for the Church as an institution, that individuals can ask some very alarming questions, and make some very disturbing statements.

- "Pastor, why is the Local Church important?"
- "Pastor, I can worship without the local church through Christian radio, television, online, and religious literature."
- "Pastor, why must a person participate in the corporate life of the Church?"
- "Pastor, it does not matter if the Church is joined, as long as I am sincere in my faith."

Such questions and statements show a fundamental disrespect to the Church, and yet, in the sight of God, the Church is still most glorious. John Newton recognized this glory when he paraphrased Psalm 87.

> Glorious things of thee are spoken,
>   Zion, city of our God;
> He whose word cannot be broken
>   formed thee for His own abode:
> On the Rock of Ages founded,
>   what can shake thy sure repose?
> With salvation's walls surrounded,
>   thou may'st smile at all thy foes.

The glory of the Church is revealed in her Divine election. "Blessed be the God and Father of our Lord Jesus Christ, who hath blessed us with all spiritual blessings in heavenly places in Christ, According as He hath chosen us in Him before the foundation of the world, that we should be holy and without blame before Him in love: Having predestinated us unto the adoption of children by Jesus Christ to Himself, according to the good pleasure of His will, To the praise of the glory of his grace, wherein He hath made us accepted in the Beloved" (Eph. 1:3–6).

The glory of the church is revealed by the great price which was paid to redeem her from the penalty, power, and pollution of sin. "In whom we have redemption through His blood, the forgiveness of sins, according to the riches of his grace" (Eph. 1:7).

The glory of the Church is seen in the adoption of those who believe, as children of God. "For ye have not received the spirit of bondage again to fear but ye have received the Spirit of adoption, whereby we cry, Abba, Father" (Rom. 8:15).

The glory of the Church is displayed in the glorious inheritance that awaits her. To the Church has been given the Kingdom of God (Luke 12:32), eternal life (Mark 10:30; John 10:28; Rom. 6:23; Heb. 9:15) and the promise of a new heaven and a new earth (2 Pet. 3:13 Rev. 21:1).

The glory of the Church is manifested in the purpose and place she has in the plan of God (Eph. 1:14). That in the ages to come He might show the exceeding riches of His grace in His kindness toward us through Christ Jesus (Eph. 3:10), to the intent that now unto the principalities and powers in heavenly places might be known by the Church the manifold wisdom of God. The

Church is no parenthetical afterthought in the mind of God. The Church occupies the pivotal place in the heart of God.

The glory of the church is reflected in the majesty of her Master, the Lord Jesus Christ, who is King of kings and Lord of lords (Col. 1:15–19; Eph. 1:22–23).

The glory of the Church may be seen in the fact that she is indwelt by God the Holy Spirit (Eph. 1:13, 17–19; 3:16). "In whom ye also trusted, after that ye heard the word of truth, the gospel of your salvation: in whom also after that ye believed, ye were sealed with that Holy Spirit of promise."

The glory of the Church may be seen in her own intrinsic holiness (Eph. 1:4; 2:10, 21; 5:26–27). "That He might sanctify and cleanse it with the washing of water by the word, That He might present it to himself a glorious church, not having spot, or wrinkle, or any such thing, but that it should be holy and without blemish."

The glory of the Church may be seen in her nearness to the presence of God (Eph. 2:13, 18; 3:12; Heb. 4:16). The Church has the ear of heaven. "Let us therefore come boldly unto the throne of grace, that we may obtain mercy, and find grace to help in time of need."

The glory of the Church may be seen in the fact that to her was entrusted the gospel (Eph. 1:9; 3:2–5). God has not entrusted the gospel to business, nor to the government, or even to religious auxiliary organizations, or specialized ministries, however good all of these things may be. The gospel is given to the Church. Only the Church has a right to say that God having "made known unto us the mystery of His will, according to His good pleasure, which He hath purposed in Himself."

I love thy Church, O God!
  Her walls before thee stand,
Dear as the apple of thine eye,
  And graven on thy hand.

For her my tears shall fall,
  For her my prayers shall ascend,
To her my cares and toils be given,
  Till toils and cares shall end.

Because the Church is glorious, it is only right that there be a definite identity with the local assembly according to the will of the Lord. Every believer should ask, How do I unite with God's people? The question should be asked because the physical unity of God's people is designed to reflect the spiritual unity that already exists.

The Bible teaches that Christians are not independent of one another. Every imagery in the Bible shows an essential unity of some sort. Whether it is the Shepherd and the Sheep, the Vine and the Branches, or the Head and the Body, the theme of unity is the same (cf. John 13:34–35; Rom. 12:5, 10, 16; 14:19; 15:14; Gal. 6:2; Eph. 4:32; 5:21; Phil. 2:3–4; 1 Thess. 4:9; 5:11; Heb. 10:24; Jas. 5:16; 1 John 4:12).

The fact that there is a spiritual unity which is designed to be manifested in the corporate life is proven by the apostles who established local churches, and gave instructions as to how they were to function and be governed (Acts 14:21–23; 1 Tim. 3:15; Titus 1:5). Pastor letters were sent to deal with specific problems, and to encourage the saints in the work of the ministry (1 Cor. 1:2; 2

Cor. 1:1; 2 Thess. 1:1). Those who unite with the local Church are entitled to several things.

Every believer is entitled to the opportunity to worship. God loves to see His people gather to praise and honor Him. The worship on earth reflects the worship of heaven itself as a gathered assembly (Heb. 12:22; Rev. 5:11–14; 7:9–12; 15:2–4; 19:1–8). Because the opportunity to worship is a gift of Divine grace, it should not be taken for granted. There is an appointed place, there is a proper time, and there is an acceptable way to worship the Lord.

Every believer is entitled to the love of the saints according to 1 Corinthians 13. Every believer is to be cared for according to the principles of mercy (Matt. 25:31–46; Acts 2:45; 4:32–35; Gal. 2:10).

Every believer is entitled to be edified in a practical manner concerning the Person and work of Jesus Christ. The Lord has given to His church pastors and teachers for the spiritual maturing of the believers (Eph. 4:8–11; 1 Pet. 2:2; Acts 20:28–32; 1 Tim. 3:2; 2 Tim. 3:16–4:4).

Every believer is entitled to enjoy Christian fellowship and encouragement (1 Cor. 12:13-27; Eph. 4:16).

Because the believer receives the gifts of God from the people of God, a holy obligation emerges when membership in the local assembly is finalized.

Those who unite with the local assembly should endeavor to be a loving person according to 1 Corinthians 13.

Those who unite with the local assembly should honor the legitimate spiritual leadership of the assembly (Heb. 13:7, 17).

Those who unite with the local assembly should seek to serve within the body of Christ (Rom. 12:4–10).

Those who unite with the local assembly should honor the terms of the Covenant and by-laws, as the congregation practices them, in order to promote peace (Rom. 14:19). Let us therefore follow after the things which make for peace, and things wherewith one may edify another.

Does this mean that all Christians will agree on every point, and on every practice? No. But there is a spirit and a mindset that allows for essential agreement so that the work of the ministry can be carried out in a Christ-like manner as best as possible.

To be specific, there are certain things that those who are strong in the faith can do for those who are weak in the faith, and there are some things that those who are weak in the faith can do for those who are strong in the faith, especially when a question arises that is controversial because it is not clear to all.

Turning to Romans 14, this point can be illustrated by the question of whether or not Jewish Christians should eat herbs, worship on special days, and eat meat that was once considered to be unclean. When some Jews were first converted to Christ, they were weak in the faith.

Stronger Christians knew that it was all right to eat herbs and meat that was once forbidden, such as pork. Those who were strong in the faith knew that the ceremonial aspect of the Law was abolished so that the seven great Jewish festival days did not have to be observed. So what was to be done with those who were weak in the faith? Paul places a burden upon those who are strong in the faith to do three things.

First, the weaker brother was to be received into the fellowship without an argument being started, or an issue being made of personal scruples (Rom. 14:1). Him that is weak in the faith receive ye, but not to doubtful disputations.

Second, the weaker brother's concerns were to be borne by those who were strong in the faith (Rom. 15:1). We then that are strong ought to bear the infirmities of the weak, and not to please ourselves. And there is a good reason why this ought to be done (Rom. 15:3). "For even Christ pleased not Himself; but, as it is written, 'The reproaches of them that reproached thee fell on me.' Because Christ has borne the sins of the saints, the saints should bear the scruples of one another with great sensitivity."

So, those who are strong in the faith are to receive those who are weak in the faith without being argumentative but with great tenderness, in order to not lay a stumbling block before them (Rom. 14:13). Let us not therefore judge one another anymore: but judge this rather, that no man put a stumbling block or an occasion to fall in his brother's way.

As those who are strong in the faith ought to do certain things for those who are weak in the faith, those who are weak in the faith also ought to do something. Specifically, there is to be a holy hush so that an inordinate amount of time is not spent judging one another in matters of personal concern (Rom. 14:10). "But why dost thou judge thy brother? Or why dost thou set at nought thy brother?"

The reason there is to be a holy hush, and a non-judgmental attitude is because we shall all stand before the judgment seat of Christ (Rom. 14:10b). "For it is written, 'As I live,' saith the Lord, 'every knee shall bow to me, and every tongue shall confess to God.' So then every one of us shall give account of himself to God" (Rom. 14:11).

When good people disagree over principles and practices, it is not to turn personal and accusatory. Rather, those who are strong in the faith are to bear the infirmities of those who are weak in the faith. And those who are weak in the faith are not to condemn those who are strong in the faith.

- A loving reception of those who are weak in the faith.
- A fundamental decision to stay together even when one does not get their way.
- A non-argumentative spirit.
- A holy hush in the sense of being non-judgmental on unclear issues.
- A willingness to wait and let each person give an account of themselves before God.
- A deliberate bearing with those who are weak in the faith.
- A pursuing of peace.

These are the things that will reflect whether a local assembly is really the Church, and different from other social institutions.

12

Judas Iscariot: The Day a Devil Died

"... and Judas Iscariot, which also was the traitor" (Luke 6:16; cf. Matt 10:4; 26:14–30; Mark 3:19).

How does an apostle of the Lord Jesus Christ become a devil? What brings a man from the highest privilege, to the lowest depths of hell? There is no easy answer to that question for the presence of moral evil in an initially perfect universe is still a great mystery. The most profound thinkers of all the ages have not been able to penetrate this great mystery. Like Adam in the Garden of Eden, Judas Iscariot fell from his exalted position. We would still like to know, Why? And, How did it happen? The facts surrounding the man are few.

We do know that the traitor's name was Judas, which was a proud and common name in Jewish history. One of the greatest patriots of the Jewish nation was Judas Maccabees. Many years before the birth of Christ, he and his brothers led a revolt against foreign oppression to liberate the Jews of his generation. In honor of Judas' great exploits, mothers named their children after him. When the wife of Simon Iscariot handed their newborn son to him (John 13:2; cf. John 6:71) for the first time, both mother and father were filled with pride. They were of the tribe of Judah. Their son should be honored with the name Judas.

Like other Jewish boys, Judas grew up with the rich tradition of Messianic expectations. The Rabbis taught from the Holy Scriptures that one day a Divine Deliverer would come and lead national Israel in a victorious revolt against foreign domination. A New Kingdom would be established and Israel would be a great world power. John the Baptist had spoken about the coming kingdom at Bethany, beyond the Jordan (John 1:28). Perhaps Judas heard the Baptist preach and his patriotic heart was stirred.

Then one day the news came. The Messiah was present. The kingdom of heaven was at hand. Multitudes flocked to hear the Young Prophet from Galilee, Jesus of Nazareth. Judas went to listen too, and remained to be numbered with the other apostles (Luke 6:12–16). What attracted Jesus and Judas to one another is not clearly revealed. Nevertheless, several things do emerge from Scripture.

First, Judas was a man with financial ability. The Bible says that he was the treasurer of the group in that he kept the purse (John 12:5–6). Matthew would have been better qualified to keep the records and count the money, but Judas was respected and trusted enough to be honored with that responsibility. Later, the truth would emerge that Judas was not worthy of the trust because he was a thief (John 12:6). Judas was a thief despite the warnings of Christ when He taught ye cannot serve God and mammon (Matt. 6:24). The Lord also asked "For what is a man profited, if he shall gain the whole world, and lose his own soul? Or what shall a man give in exchange for his soul" (Matt. 16:26)?

Second, Judas was an apostle. He had been empowered to preach the gospel. He had been given authority to heal the sick and cast out devils (Mark 3:14–19). He who had no saving grace could still be a source of blessing to others.

Third, Judas was a man of persuasive reasoning, reflected by a scene in the home of Mary of Bethany. Mary had anointed Jesus with a rich ointment. She did this by faith in preparation for the Lord's date with death (John 12:7). Judas saw the act of love as a waste of precious money, and found a way to say so with clever words. Why was not this ointment sold for three hundred shillings and given to the poor (John 12:5)?

When Peter, James, John, and the other disciples heard the remark, it struck a note of simple logic in their heart, and they too joined in. Why this waste? They cried, forgetting that it is never a waste to perform spiritual acts of worship.

Fourth, Judas was a man of good reputation. He was above suspicion by the other disciples up to the final hours of his own life. At the Last Supper it was Judas who sat in the place of honor. He reclined near the Lord on the left so that they could talk quietly. When Jesus said, One of you shall betray me, no one even looked at Judas in suspicion (John 13:21).

The composite picture of Judas as an ordained apostle of financial competence with persuasive verbal abilities, and the persona to command personal respect has compelled some bible students to have compassion for him. More than one religious writer has tried to portray Judas as almost virtuous. Thomas de Quincey in an essay on Judas Iscariot has tried to present him as merely a misguided patriot. Quincey naively argues that Judas actually loved Jesus and only hung himself because his scheme did not materialize for forcing Jesus into political leadership against Rome.

Partial evidence to support this view is said to be found in the word used for kiss in the gospels (Matt. 26:47–50; Mark 14:43–45; and Luke 22:47). The word kiss is *kataphileiō*, which means to kiss fondly and repeatedly. It was the custom of that day for a disciple, when he met a Rabbi, to place his hands on the Rabbi's shoulders and to kiss him. When Judas met Jesus in the Garden, he kissed him again and again with eyes alighted and a quickened heartbeat. The idea is presented that when Judas kissed Jesus, he was kissing him with great excitement believing that he had finally found a way to force the Lord to act. Judas thought that the Lord must use His Divine power to resist arrest and defend Himself. This use of divine power would naturally lead to a national uprising against Rome. But the whole scheme failed.

The main problem with this reconstruction of the mental state and motives of Judas is that it makes the Lord's death an accident, and Judas somewhat noble. If the heart of Judas was only mistaken patriotic zeal, that is one thing; if his heart was stained with sin, that is something else.

Other motives have been suggested as to why Judas betrayed Jesus. Mark Rutherford suggests that Judas used his reason in a clear-sighted and cool manner to discern that the ministry of Christ was all over. Because Judas foresaw a head-on collision with the Roman authorities he simply arranged to have the Lord arrested, not to have Christ killed, but to have Him taken out of harm's way. Judas sought to protect Jesus before ultimate injury could come to the Master.

Rutherford concludes his discussion on Judas by lamenting that later on, after the crucifixion and after Judas had committed suicide, no witnesses were ever called on Judas' behalf, and Judas never told his own story. But perhaps this should have been done. What would his friends of Kerrioth have said for him? What would Jesus have said? If he had met Judas with the halter in his hand, would he not have stopped him? Ah! I can see the divine touch on the shoulder, the passionate prostration of the repentant in the dust, the hands gently lifting him, the forgiveness for he knew not what he did, and the seal of a kiss indeed from the sacred lips.

Certainly one of the loveliest and most gracious things that was ever said by any preacher or commentator about Judas was said by the second century Greek teacher and church father, Origen (c. A.D. 85–254). Origen suggested that as soon as Judas fully realized just what he had done, he rushed to commit suicide in order to meet the Lord in Hades, the place of all the dead, and there beg the Lord's forgiveness.

While all the efforts to redeem the reputation of Judas are thoughtful, there are serious problems with the attempts to find virtue and nobility in the man. First, there are the words of Jesus. In Matthew 26:24, the Lord spoke of the traitor, and said, It would have been good had he never been born. In John 6:70, the Christ revealed, Have I not chosen you twelve and yet one of you is a devil? And Jesus knew which one was a devil. A year before he was arrested Jesus was calling Judas diabolic because He knew who should betray Him (cf. John 2:24–25; 6:64). Professor A. B. Bruce plainly writes, that, Iscariot was chosen merely to be a traitor, as an actor might be chosen to play the part of Iago (cf. Jude 1:4). And the Scriptures of prophecy were fulfilled. Psalm 41:9, "Yea, mine own familiar friend, in whom I trusted, which did eat of my bread, hath lifted up his heel against me."

Looking at the motive of betrayal by Judas with a critical eye, several possibilities emerge. It may be that Judas was a man who was always on the outside looking in. We have already noticed how Judas was trusted by the other apostles, and was influential over them. But Judas was not among the most intimate of the group, as Peter, James, and John. Judas might have felt that one reason for this was social prejudice. He was from Kerioth, in the district of Jerusalem, while the other disciples were from Galilee. There was a natural tension and mistrust between the two people in the geographical locations. Dr. William Barclay comments: "It is not difficult to see him, even if he had a high place among the Twelve, slowly and unreasonably growing jealous and embittered because others had a still higher place. And it is not difficult to see that bitterness coming to obsess him, until in the end his love turned to hate and he betrayed Jesus."

There is a second motive that could have driven Judas to betray Jesus, and that is simply an insatiable love for money. The Bible tells us that love of money is the root of all forms of evil (1 Tim. 6:10). In John 12:1–8 the Scriptures record that Judas carried the money bag. The Greek word is *bastazein*, which could mean to embezzle. To lift or bear a thing can mean to carry it or it can mean to steal something, as in the word shoplifter. Perhaps

Judas was robbing from the purse. If money was Judas' motive for the betrayal, he sold his immortal soul very cheaply. Thirty pieces of silver is only worth about $100.00.

In the final analysis, the primary influence upon the will of Judas to inflame his inner motive was not spite, jealousy, money, or political ambition, but Satan himself. Satan, says Luke, entered into Judas (Luke 22:3). As John tells the story, it was at the Last Supper that the Evil One took final possession of the soul of Judas and he went out into the night to betray the Light of the World (John 13:2; cf. John 6:70).

The ability of Satan to literally possess Judas is a difficult concept to understand, but there are some things that help, beginning with the fact that the Bible teaches there is another form of life called angels. There are two types of angels: the fallen, and the elect (Jude 1:6). Fallen angels, led by Lucifer, are called demons. Demons have a fascination with mortals, for they desire to possess human bodies. One thing that keeps the demons from being more influential are the prayers of the Lord for His own. Without the prayers of the Lord, Christians would be open to demon infiltration. Judas was not only open to demonic infiltration, he was inhabited by the Ruler of Darkness himself. However, it is possible that Judas was not Satan's first choice of occupancy.

Luke records an incident where Jesus speaks to Peter saying, "Simon, Simon, behold Satan hath desired to have you, that he may sift you as wheat" (22:31). The only thing that kept Simon Peter safe from Satan was the Lord's Prayer. But I have prayed for thee, that thy faith fail not; and when thou art converted strengthen thy brethren. Jesus never prayed for Judas the same way He prayed for Peter. In fact, in John 17, the Lord prayed for all of the disciples except one, the Son of Perdition, that the Scripture might be fulfilled (17:12).

In the fullness of time, according to the Sovereign will of God, Jesus was born to bear the sins of the saints. And in the fullness of time, according to the providence of God, Judas was also born to fulfill the Scriptures. The Bible teaches that God works all things according to the counsel of His own will (Eph. 1:11). Individuals are free to be what the Lord enables them to be. Apart from the Lord, individuals are also free to be what the world, the flesh, and the devil wants them to be. Jesus said, "You have not chosen me but I have chosen you, and one of you is a devil."

From a human perspective, Judas betrayed Jesus from a mixture of personal motives, to include being a misguided patriot, harboring petty bitterness, while trying to satisfy an insatiable love for money. These factors were used by Satan to compel Judas to intentionally betray Christ. It was not an irrational response to an isolated emotional situation that caused Judas to become traitorous. Matthew 26:16 tells us "He sought opportunity to betray Him." And Mark 14:11 records that "He sought how he might conveniently betray Him." All of this is from a human viewpoint.

From a divine perspective, Judas betrayed Jesus in order that the Scriptures might be fulfilled. In all of this, there is a great mystery, for it is not easy to discern where human responsibility and divine sovereignty unite. The late John F. Kennedy Jr once asked the late Rev. Billy Graham about this for an interview with *George* magazine. He asked if people were always responsible for their actions or is there a time when the Divine will supersedes. Dr. Graham acknowledged that the question delves into a great mystery, for both things are true: God is sovereign and men are responsible for what they do and say.

The acceptance of personal responsibility for his actions is manifested in the life of Judas in that he felt remorse. In the end, Judas was not without sorrow and grief. Running back to the Temple with a growing horror, Judas cast the money of betrayal back in the face of the priests (Matt. 27:1–4) while crying with shame, I have sinned. I have betrayed innocent blood.

> Thirty pieces of silver burns on the traitor's brain,
> Thirty pieces of silver—oh, it is hellish gain:
> I have sinned and betrayed the guiltless,
> He cried with a lowered breath,
> As he threw them down in the Temple
> And rushed to a madman's death.
>
> —W. Blane

Temporal death was followed by eternal death. There was no one present to say, "Son, thy sins be forgiven thee." Sometimes repentance comes too late. Sometimes, there is a point of no return. There is an invisible line that can be crossed in which there is no hope of salvation or coming to repentance. Judas crossed the line and he knew it. And so it was that Judas went out and hung himself. When the rope broke, he fell upon jagged rocks where his body burst open. "Truly it would have been better for that man if he had never been born" (Matt. 26:24, NEB). The final word on Judas is found in Acts where it is recorded that he went to his own place (Acts 1:25). Judas went from the hallowed place in the Garden of Gethsemane to the hellish place where the worm dieth not and the fire is not quenched. And the question comes, Where is your place? Is it at Gethsemane with Jesus or in Gehenna with Judas?

> It may not be for silver, it may not be for gold,
>> But yet by tens of thousands the Prince of Life is sold,
> Sold for a godless friendship, sold for a selfish aim,
>> Sold for a fleeting trifle, sold for an empty name.
>
> Sold in the mart of science, sold in the seat of power,
>> Sold at the shrine of fortune, sold in pleasure's arbor,
> Sold for an awful bargain none but God's eye can see,
>> Ponder my soul the question, shall He be sold by thee?
>
> Sold! Oh God, what a moment! Stilled is conscience voice;
>> Sold! And a weeping angel records the fatal choice,
> Sold! But the price accepted to a living coal shall turn,
>> With the pangs of a late repentance deep in the soul to burn.
>
> Heaven or hell. Paradise or perdition—
>> The choice is made this side of the grave.
>> —Dr. Herbert Lockyer

The Apostles' Creed[7]

I believe in God, the Father Almighty,
the Creator of heaven and earth,
and in Jesus Christ,
His only Son, our Lord:

Who was conceived of the Holy Spirit,
born of the Virgin Mary,
suffered under Pontius Pilate,
was crucified, died, and was buried.
He descended into hell.

The third day He arose again from the dead.
He ascended into heaven
and sits at the right hand of God the Father Almighty,
whence He shall come to judge the living and the dead.

I believe in the Holy Spirit,
the holy catholic [universal] church,
the communion of saints,

---

[7] One of the earliest confessions of faith is called The Apostles' Creed. It has received this title because of its great age; it dates from very early times in the Church, a half-century or so from the last writings of the New Testament.

the forgiveness of sins,
the resurrection of the body,
and life everlasting."

AMEN.